P9-DEG-269

TECHNOLOGY

Britannica Illustrated Science Library

Encyclopædia Britannica, Inc.

Chicago ■ London ■ New Delhi ■ Paris ■ Seoul ■ Sydney ■ Taipei ■ Tokyo

Britannica Illustrated Science Library

Idea and Concept of This Work: Editorial Sol 90

Project Management: Fabián Cassan

Photo Credits: Corbis

Composition and Pre-press Services: Editorial Sol 90

Translation Services and Index: Publication Services, Inc.

International Standard Book Number (set):
    978-1-59339-382-3
International Standard Book Number (volume):
    978-1-59339-398-4
Britannica Illustrated Science Library: Technology 2008

Printed in China

ENCYCLOPÆDIA
Britannica®

www.britannica.com

Technology

Contents

NANOROBOT
Microscopic device that is formed by arms scarcely 10 nanometers in length. In the photograph, it is shown transporting a drug through the interior of an infected cell.

An Endless Inventiveness

M any animal species use tools, and some, such as crows and apes, can even create them. But only our species has taken this ability to such an extreme that it can be said that we maintain an evolutionary symbiosis with these tools. In other words, our ability to develop complex tools increased our intelligence, allowing us to manufacture even more complex tools. This, in turn, launched a new phase in this cycle, and after several million years it finally led to the modern human, who continues to develop tools that will likely continue to transform the species. Of course, this history has not always followed a linear path. In the 9,000 years since humans discovered agriculture and cattle farming, many inventions were discovered many times and forgotten nearly as many times. Today we are surprised to learn that the Romans knew about concrete and that they had taxis and hamburger stands or that the Greeks developed the basic principles of the locomotive and the steam engine (although, oddly enough, they never combined the two to invent the railroad). We have developed the most absurd theories to explain the construction of the pyramids in Egypt or the moai of Easter Island. This winding history, with steps forward and steps backward, can be explained thus: technical inventions are a specific response to the specific needs of a given human group, and when these needs or the people who needed to meet those needs disappear or change, the inventions associated with them also disappear or change.

A few centuries ago, the creative ability of human beings took a major leap forward when tools associated with craft and empirical techniques began to complement science, thus systematizing the methods of production. This is how modern technology emerged, allowing improved preservation not just of know-how but also of the economic, social, and cultural aspects involving this know-how. Once tool making ceased to be something that was passed on from master craftsman to apprentice and became an organized set of procedures and knowledge accessible to a specialized community, the human ability to invent new tools underwent an explosion similar to the one it experienced 9,000 years earlier. Virtually overnight thousands of objects appeared (and would continue to appear) that changed our way of seeing and understanding the world—the clock, which allowed us to divide time and set a new pace for our lives; the printing press, which allowed knowledge to be spread beyond a privileged few; the refrigerator, which enriched and diversified our nutrition practices; the cinema, which opened up the possibility of dreaming while awake; the Internet, which erased borders and distances; and robotics and artificial intelligence, which led us to question our definition of being human. With the emergence of technology, you could say that our lives are surrounded by marvelous objects.

This book takes us on a journey through some of the inventions that have changed our everyday habits and our understanding of the world that surrounds us. It is not meant to provide a thorough or definitive view. The creative abilities of human beings will always make such a task incomplete. Here we look at the revolutionary technologies that mark milestones in the development of technology. We also examine inventions that have become so essential in our daily lives that it is difficult to imagine the way the world was prior to their existence. We look at technologies that have lengthened our life expectancy and improved our health. We also explore inventions that are just now beginning to show their potential and are opening up worlds that not even the most imaginative science-fiction authors could have foreseen. It is surprising to see the degree to which many of these technologies are related, like a rich tapestry of invention and creativity that make us grow as a species, expand our culture, satisfy our needs, and shape us as a society. ●

Daily-Life Applications

Technology has been an integral part of our daily lives for several decades now, drastically affecting us in many positive ways. Liquid crystal displays (LCD) form a part of a plethora of industrial and consumer appliances, such as automated teller machines, home appliances, television equipment, and computers. The

scanner, calculator, and fax revolutionized the worlds of work and study, and photography, the DVD, and the camcorder allowed us to stop time and save unique moments forever. Our daily lives are altered by technology. We see it wherever we look; it offers us the things we have always sought: comfort, entertainment, and the tools to make our daily tasks easier. ●

The iPod

This fifth-generation, sophisticated multimedia player, introduced by Apple in 2001, currently lets users store and play up to 80 GB of music, video, and images, encoded in many formats; it also allows them to transfer information from both Mac and PC computers. The iPod can download new files from iTunes, an exchange software developed by Apple. This software serves as a complex data manager, allowing customers to purchase files from a library of more than 3 million songs and 3,000 videos. ●

Endless Entertainment

One of the most notable features of the attractively designed iPod is its ability to store high-fidelity recordings. In a size slightly larger than the palm of a person's hand, users can store up to 80 GB of data.

Music
The iPod can store more than 20,000 songs in its 80 GB version (and up to 7,000 songs in its 30 GB version).

Video
The 80 GB version can store and play more than 100 hours of video in various file formats.

Games
The iPod comes with four games, but it is possible to download a large number of games from iTunes.

5 GB iPod

4 inches (10.4 cm)

2.4 inches (6.1 cm)

Images
Stores more than 25,000 images. Plugged into a home theater system, it can display the images with musical accompaniment on a large screen.

Evolution

Since its launch in 2001, the iPod has become smaller, lighter, and more efficient. It now has a color screen, and its maximum storage capacity is 16 times greater than the first model. The iPod spawned a flourishing business in accessories, and it has become a symbol of an entire generation. Today it is the most popular portable multimedia player.

2001	2004	2004	2005	2005	2005	2007
Original iPod	**Mini iPod**	**U2 iPod**	**iPod Nano**	**iPod Shuffle**	**5G iPod**	**iPod Touch**
The first version of the iPod held 5 GB of information.	Up to 6 GB capacity. Discontinued.	This model was launched in partnership with the band U2 and Universal Music Group.	The successor of the iPod mini. Smaller and lighter, with a color screen. Holds up to 8 GB.	The smallest model, it weighs only 0.5 ounce (15 g) and has no screen.	Holds up to 80 GB; 2.5-inch (6.3-cm) color screen.	A touch screen in full color with access to YouTube

Complexity in a Small Container

The interior of a 2 GB iPod Nano illustrates the complexity of this multimedia player. Chips, circuits, plates, ports, and even a thin liquid crystal display fit into a space only 3.5 x 1.5 inches (9 x 4 cm).

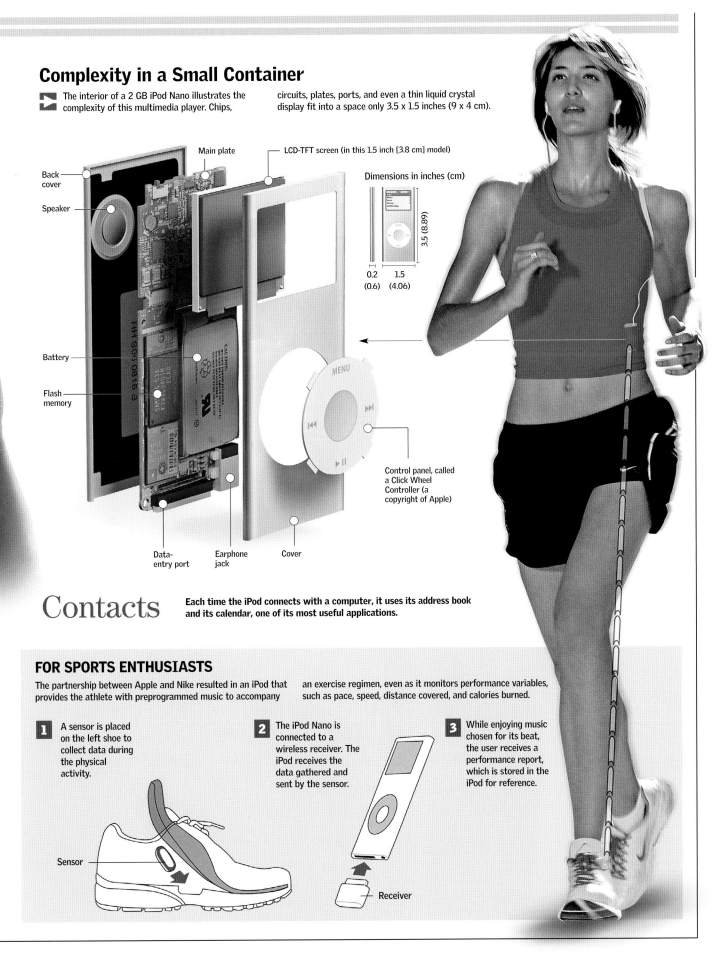

Back cover

Main plate

LCD-TFT screen (in this 1.5 inch [3.8 cm] model)

Speaker

Dimensions in inches (cm)

3.5 (8.89)

0.2 (0.6) 1.5 (4.06)

Battery

Flash memory

MENU

Control panel, called a Click Wheel Controller (a copyright of Apple)

Data-entry port

Earphone jack

Cover

Contacts

Each time the iPod connects with a computer, it uses its address book and its calendar, one of its most useful applications.

FOR SPORTS ENTHUSIASTS

The partnership between Apple and Nike resulted in an iPod that provides the athlete with preprogrammed music to accompany an exercise regimen, even as it monitors performance variables, such as pace, speed, distance covered, and calories burned.

1 A sensor is placed on the left shoe to collect data during the physical activity.

2 The iPod Nano is connected to a wireless receiver. The iPod receives the data gathered and sent by the sensor.

3 While enjoying music chosen for its beat, the user receives a performance report, which is stored in the iPod for reference.

Sensor

Receiver

LCDs

The technology used in the displays of small cell phones and laptops is based on the use of liquid crystals—a discovery dating back to the 19th century. This technology has been applied to television sets, causing a revolution in terms of size and image quality. LCD televisions are flatter and lighter than conventional sets and need less power to operate. ●

INSIDE THE SCREEN

LED BULBS

State-of-the-art screens use diodes, which emit red, green, and blue light. Together these colors form a powerful white light that replaces traditional fluorescent tubes.

DIFFUSER

controls brightness and softens the light.

CIRCUITS

convert the TV signal into electric instructions for the liquid crystal to use in forming the image on the screen.

LIQUID CRYSTAL

Discovered at the end of the 19th century, liquid crystals share characteristics of both solids and liquids. Their molecules can have a specific crystalline structure—which is characteristic of solids— but still have some freedom of movement. In LCDs, crystals can be oriented by electric impulses while staying in place.

THE IMAGE

is formed by hundreds of thousands of points of light called pixels. The color and intensity of each pixel is controlled by the combined brightness of the red, blue, and green subpixels.

The color of each pixel depends upon the brightness of each subpixel.

● + ● + ● = ○ The mixture of the three subpixels at maximum brightness produces white light.

○ + ○ + ○ = ● If the three subpixels are dimmed completely, the pixel becomes black.

The Path of the Light

▶ Inside an LCD screen, white light is turned into a TV image with the help of polarizers, microscopic crystals, and color filters. Much of the process depends on technology that orients the light rays in a precise manner. From an environmental point of view, LCD screens emit almost no electromagnetic radiation, and their energy consumption can be less than 60 percent of what the cathode-ray tube of a conventional television set requires.

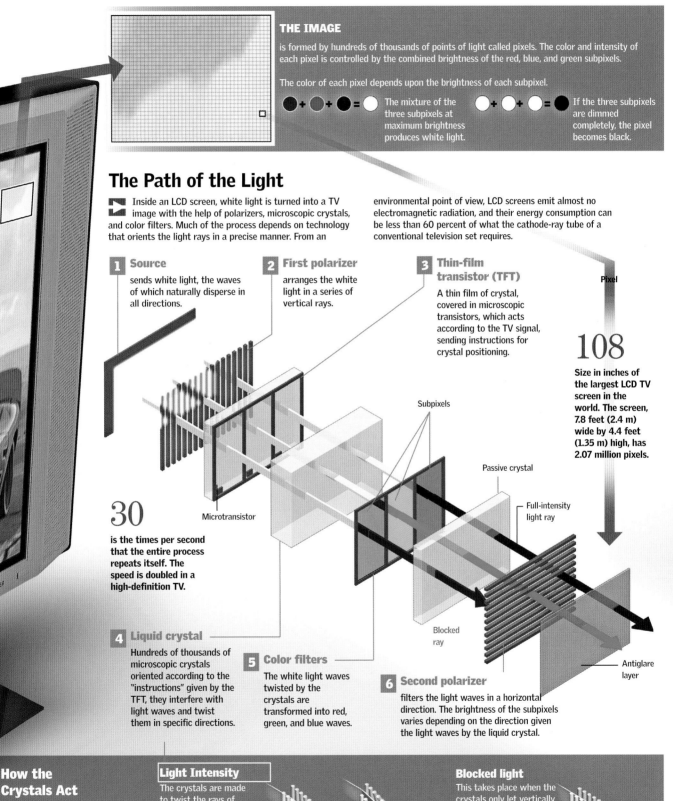

1 Source
sends white light, the waves of which naturally disperse in all directions.

2 First polarizer
arranges the white light in a series of vertical rays.

3 Thin-film transistor (TFT)
A thin film of crystal, covered in microscopic transistors, which acts according to the TV signal, sending instructions for crystal positioning.

Pixel

108

Size in inches of the largest LCD TV screen in the world. The screen, 7.8 feet (2.4 m) wide by 4.4 feet (1.35 m) high, has 2.07 million pixels.

Subpixels

Passive crystal

Full-intensity light ray

30

is the times per second that the entire process repeats itself. The speed is doubled in a high-definition TV.

Microtransistor

4 Liquid crystal
Hundreds of thousands of microscopic crystals oriented according to the "instructions" given by the TFT, they interfere with light waves and twist them in specific directions.

5 Color filters
The white light waves twisted by the crystals are transformed into red, green, and blue waves.

6 Second polarizer
filters the light waves in a horizontal direction. The brightness of the subpixels varies depending on the direction given the light waves by the liquid crystal.

Blocked ray

Antiglare layer

How the Crystals Act

The voltage applied to the crystals by the TFT forces them to change their alignment, twisting the light that passes through them.

Light Intensity
The crystals are made to twist the rays of light. The light's final brightness depends on how horizontal the rays are.

Medium intensity   Full intensity

Blocked light
This takes place when the crystals only let vertically oriented light waves through, which are then blocked by the second horizontal polarizer.

3-D Movies

The recent appearance of 3-D movie theaters with IMAX technology put the public in touch with new ideas in cinematography. The images' high resolution and large size (exceeding human peripheral vision), combined with high-quality sound and three-dimensional effects, attempt to immerse viewers within a movie. At first, only documentary films were shown in these theaters, because special filming systems were required. However, in recent years, more and more commercial films have been produced in this format.

The Theater

IMAX movie-projection rooms are characterized by their large screen size and their high-quality sound. These two elements, combined with 3-D effects, immerse viewers in the movie.

is the average weight of an IMAX film reel. Operators must handle them with cranes.

Projector
has two lenses whose images converge on the screen. Two 15,000-watt lamps are necessary to light such a large screen.

Cooling hoses and pipes

Sound system
Separated into six channels and one subwoofer, for realistic audio

Platters
The two reels display the same movie, from two slightly divergent angles, imitating the human field of vision. They are projected simultaneously.

Filming for IMAX

To achieve 3-D effects, two cameras are used in IMAX filming. Each camera corresponds to a different eye, with the angle of separation reproducing the angle of separation between human eyes.

Because the two cameras cannot be placed close enough to achieve the 3-D effect, a mirror is used to resolve the problem.

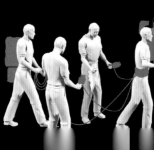

Camera

Semitransparent mirror

Camera

The 3-D Effect

uses two lenses to converge images on the screen. Each lens corresponds to the angle of vision of one of the eyes, and each projection is polarized at an angle perpendicular to the other.

1 Each projector lens polarizes the image at an angle perpendicular to the other.

Horizontal polarization (left eye)

Vertical polarization (right eye)

Comparison with 35-mm Movies

▶ The greatest achievement of IMAX theater in comparison to traditional movie theaters is the size and quality of the images projected, combined with the sound system and 3-D effects.

THE SCREEN

These are the largest screens in the movie industry. They are more than 65 feet (20 m) wide, and the high-resolution projection produces excellent image quality. Because they surpass the normal range of human peripheral vision, viewers feel completely immersed in the film.

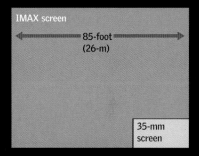

IMAX screen
◀――――――― 85-foot ―――――――▶
(26-m)

35-mm screen

THE FILM

Each frame measures 1.9 by 2.7 inches (50 by 70 mm) and has 15 perforations. In other words, it has 10 times the surface area of the 35-mm film used in traditional projections. Each image corresponds to two frames filmed from slightly different angles, producing a 3-D effect. Unlike conventional movies, the film moves through the projector horizontally— and at much greater speed.

70-mm film

35-mm film

Screen
Of great size and slightly concave

Projection Theaters

▶ IMAX technology allows for two types of theaters: the traditional type with a large, flat screen, and dome-shaped rooms, in which the projection extends to the sides and ceiling.

② The eyeglasses used by viewers have perpendicular polarizers corresponding to those of the projector's lenses.

③ Thus, during the projection of the movie, the polarizers of each eye allow the corresponding image through, blocking the image intended for the other eye.

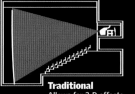

Traditional
Allows for 3-D effects

Dome
The viewer feels immersed within the film. No 3-D effects.

The DVD

T he storage capacity of a DVD, six times that of a traditional CD, has revolutionized the way digital data is organized and stored in the decade since its appearance in 1997. The DVD explosion resounded in the world of home movies thanks to its capability of storing entire feature films, bonus material, and subtitles (in various languages) on only one disc. The evolution of technology, however, has not stopped with DVDs. Recent years have seen the introduction of discs able to hold 12 times the data of the DVD. ●

Reading with Light

Optical discs (CDs and DVDs) are read by a laser beam to obtain information. This information is transformed into a binary electric signal that is later interpreted and converted into sounds, images, and data.

1 Laser emitter
generates a laser beam of a specific wavelength.

2 Mirrors
guide the ray by working in coordination.

3 Direction
In order to read the disc, the laser beam must strike the surface of the disc perpendicularly.

4 Lens
focuses the laser beam before it reaches the surface of the disc.

5 Reading
The laser beam strikes the disc's reflective surface. The reflection varies according to the pattern of pits on the disc's surface.

6 Prism
changes the direction of the laser beam that reflects from the disc and contains the data read from the disc.

7 Photodiodes
translate the variations in the returning laser beam and convert them into a digital signal.

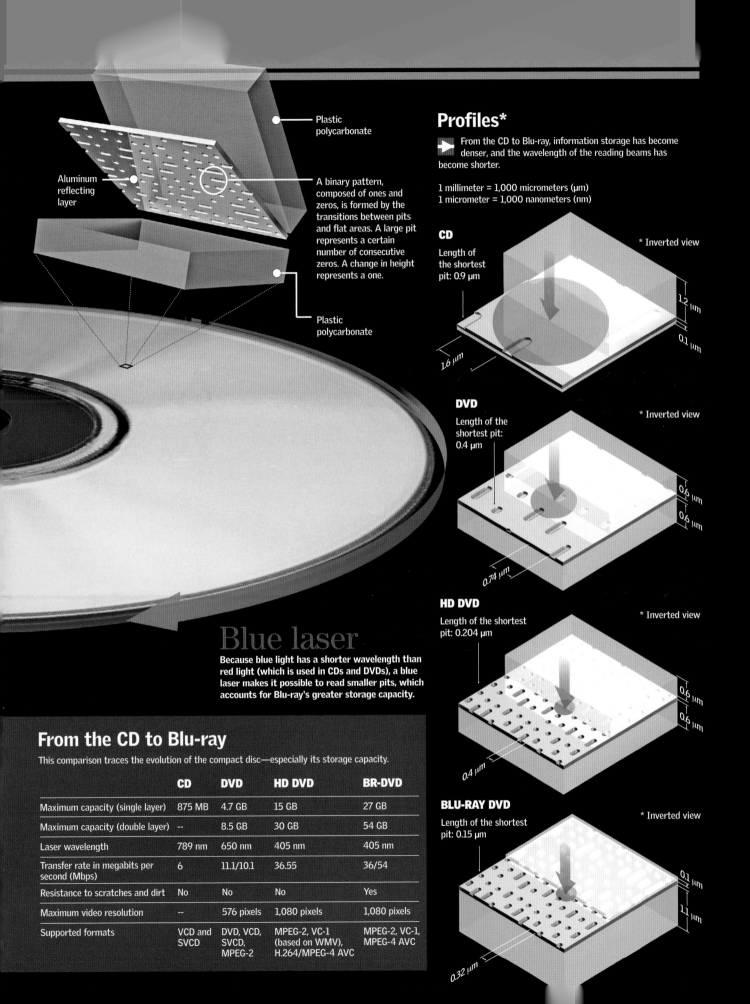

Plastic
polycarbonate

Aluminum
reflecting
layer

A binary pattern,
composed of ones and
zeros, is formed by the
transitions between pits
and flat areas. A large pit
represents a certain
number of consecutive
zeros. A change in height
represents a one.

Plastic
polycarbonate

Profiles*

From the CD to Blu-ray, information storage has become denser, and the wavelength of the reading beams has become shorter.

1 millimeter = 1,000 micrometers (μm)
1 micrometer = 1,000 nanometers (nm)

CD
Length of the shortest pit: 0.9 μm

* Inverted view

1.2 μm
0.1 μm
1.6 μm

DVD
Length of the shortest pit: 0.4 μm

* Inverted view

0.6 μm
0.6 μm
0.74 μm

HD DVD
Length of the shortest pit: 0.204 μm

* Inverted view

0.6 μm
0.6 μm
0.4 μm

BLU-RAY DVD
Length of the shortest pit: 0.15 μm

* Inverted view

0.1 μm
1.1 μm
0.32 μm

Blue laser

Because blue light has a shorter wavelength than red light (which is used in CDs and DVDs), a blue laser makes it possible to read smaller pits, which accounts for Blu-ray's greater storage capacity.

From the CD to Blu-ray

This comparison traces the evolution of the compact disc—especially its storage capacity.

	CD	DVD	HD DVD	BR-DVD
Maximum capacity (single layer)	875 MB	4.7 GB	15 GB	27 GB
Maximum capacity (double layer)	--	8.5 GB	30 GB	54 GB
Laser wavelength	789 nm	650 nm	405 nm	405 nm
Transfer rate in megabits per second (Mbps)	6	11.1/10.1	36.55	36/54
Resistance to scratches and dirt	No	No	No	Yes
Maximum video resolution	--	576 pixels	1,080 pixels	1,080 pixels
Supported formats	VCD and SVCD	DVD, VCD, SVCD, MPEG-2	MPEG-2, VC-1 (based on WMV), H.264/MPEG-4 AVC	MPEG-2, VC-1, MPEG-4 AVC

Nintendo Wii

With the launch of Wii, Nintendo tried to cause a revolution in the world of video-game consoles. Wii, the fifth generation of Nintendo's video-game consoles and part of the seventh generation of video gaming, is the successor to Nintendo's GameCube. Wii has several features intended to help a wider audience play video games and get closer to the world of virtual reality. Among them are sophisticated wireless commands that transfer tactile effects, such as blows and vibrations; infrared sensors that detect the position of the player in a room and convey the information to the console; and separate controls for each hand. Wii was a commercial success from the moment of its launch in December 2006. ●

The Console

is the brain of Wii. Its slim design (a mere 1.7 inches [4.4 cm] wide) plays the games that are loaded on standard 4.7-inch (12-cm) discs, accepting both single- and double-layered discs.

System

has an IBM PowerPC processor, ports for four controllers, two USB ports, slots for memory expansion, stereo sound, and support for playing videos on panoramic 16:9 screens.

Connectivity

The console connects with the Internet (it includes Wi-Fi wireless connection), from which it can receive updates 24 hours a day to add or upgrade features.

Console

Infrared sensor

detects the player's position from up to a distance of 32 feet (10 m) or 16 feet (5 m) during use of the pointer function (used to indicate points on the screen).

32 feet (10 m)

250,000

Wii consoles are manufactured daily by Nintendo. In preparation for the Wii's launch in Japan, 400,000 units were manufactured (an unprecedented quantity for a new console), all of which were sold within a few hours.

The Wiimote

The Wiimote, the Wii's remote, differs from traditional game consoles by looking more like a remote control than a videogame controller. It was developed to be useable with just one hand.

The Movement Sensor

A player's movements are detected by means of a flexible silicon bar inside the Wiimote. This bar moves within an electric field generated by capacitors. The player's movements cause the bar to change the electric field. The change is detected and transmitted to the infrared sensor, which translates it into the movements of the virtual character.

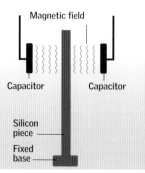

Magnetic field

Capacitor   Capacitor

Silicon piece

Fixed base

Magnetic field

Silicon piece

Fixed base

Movement

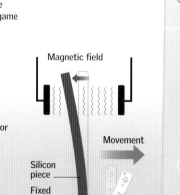

Vibrator
generates vibrations appropriate for the situation, such as when shooting a gun or hitting a ball.

Internal speaker
reproduces sounds, such as gunshots or the clash of swords.

Console buttons (holding down both buttons activates Wiimote's discovery mode, which can be used to set it up to work with a Bluetooth-enabled PC)

LED light
indicates which player is active in multiplayer games.

Players

Up to four players can participate simultaneously in the same game. All of the sensors use Bluetooth wireless technology.

Enthusiasm

The "excessive enthusiasm" of some early players caused worries about the weakness of Wiimote straps, so Nintendo decided to replace them with safer ones and modified 3,200,000 units.

Security strap
allows for the safe use of the controller with one hand, keeping the Wiimote from falling or slipping.

Controllers for every occasion

Infrared emitter

Button

Dimensions

POWER

5.8 inches (14.8 cm)

Wii

1.2 inches (3.08 cm)

1.4 inches (3.62 cm)

Port is used to add peripherals, such as the Nunchuck, which not only enhances its functions but also its traditional controller.

Nunchuck

It is connected to the Wiimote and introduces additional options for specific games, such as two-handed boxing or changing viewpoints in target shooting.

Wii

Traditional controller

Wii

This controller is still necessary for playing with games from earlier Nintendo consoles.

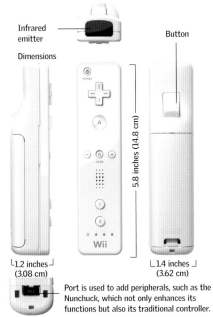

The Digital Camera

The word "photography" comes from Greek words which, combined, mean "to draw with light" (from *photos*, or "light," and *graphis*, or "drawing"). Photography is the technique of recording fixed images on a light-sensitive surface. Digital cameras are based on the principles of traditional photography, but, instead of fixing images on film coated with chemical substances sensitive to light, they process the intensity of the light and store the data in digital files. Modern digital cameras generally have multiple functions and are able to record sound and video in addition to photographs. ●

The Digital System

1 IMAGE CAPTURE

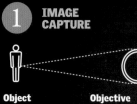

Digital image
The image appears upside down and laterally inverted.

Object

Objective
The objective focuses the image, refracting the light rays that arrive from the object so that they converge into a coherent image.

Diaphragm
It determines the amount of light that enters through the lens. This is measured in f-numbers. The greater the f-number, the smaller the opening of the diaphragm.

Shutter
The shutter determines the length of the exposure. It is generally measured in fractions of a second. The faster the shutter, the shorter the exposure.

CCD

THE SENSOR THAT REPLACES FILM

The CCD (charge-coupled device) is a group of small diodes sensitive to light (photosites), which convert photons (light) into electrons (electric charges).

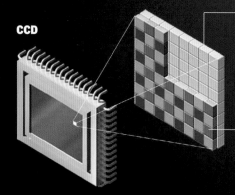

CCD

Photosites
are light-sensitive cells. The amount of light shining on the photosites is directly proportional to the electric charge that is accumulated.

Filters
To generate a color image, a series of filters must unpack the image into discrete values of red, green, and blue (RGB).

A Long Evolution

The camera obscura

Light rays reflected by an object pass through a tiny hole and are projected as an inverted image within a box. A lens concentrates the light and focuses the image. Mirrors are used to reflect the image on a flat surface, and an artist traces the projected image.

1500

A light-sensitive substance

Experiments by the German scientist Frederick Schulze prove that light blackens silver nitrate.

1725

The optical and chemical principles are combined.

Images are created by placing sheets directly over the light-sensitive paper and exposing them to sunlight. The images cannot be fixed.

1802

Nicéphore Niépce

exposes a tin plate, covered with bitumen, to light for eight hours. The bitumen hardens and turns white from the exposure, producing an image. The non-hardened areas are then washed away.

1826

The daguerreotype

The daguerreotype obtained finely detailed images on copper plates covered with silver and photosensitized with iodine. The images (single and positive) are developed with mercury vapor and fixed with saline solution.

1839

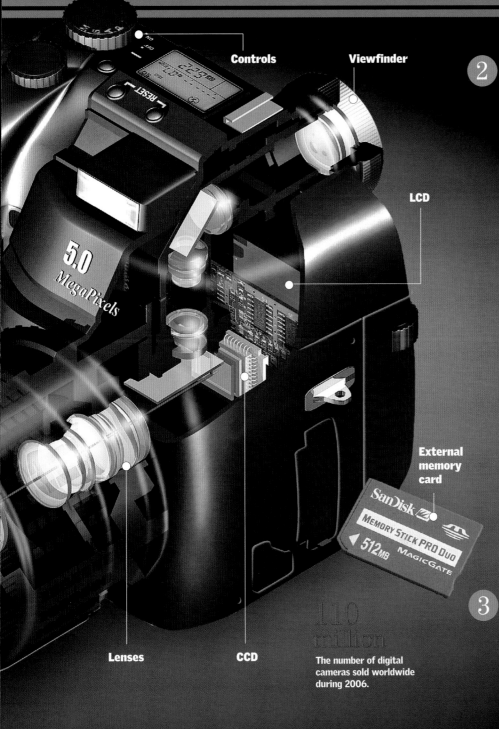

Controls

Viewfinder

LCD

5.0 MegaPixels

External memory card

SanDisk
MEMORY STICK PRO DUO
MAGICGATE
512MB

Lenses

CCD

110 million

The number of digital cameras sold worldwide during 2006.

② Binary system processing

To convert the electric charges of the photosite (analog) to digital signals, the camera uses a converter (ADC), which assigns a binary value to each one of the charges stored in the photosite, storing them as pixels (points of color).

ADDITIVE MIXTURE

Each pixel is colored by mixing values of RGB. Varying quantities of each of these colors can reproduce almost any color of the visible spectrum.

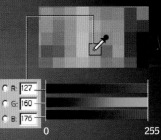

C R: 127
C G: 160
C B: 176

0   255

The value of each can vary from 0 (darkness) to 255 (the greatest color intensity).

RESOLUTION

is measured in PPIs, or pixels per square inch— the number of pixels that can be captured by a digital camera. This figure indicates the size and quality of the image.

③ Compression and storage

Once the image is digitized, a microprocessor compresses the data in memory as JPG or TIFF files.

The calotype
Invented by Talbot, this is the first positive-to-negative process. The exposures last from one to five minutes. An unlimited number of prints could be reproduced from a single negative.

1841

Glass plates
The substitution of paper for a glass plate is perfected. The plates are sensitized with silver nitrate, which received the negative image. The exposure is only a few seconds.

1851

In color
The Scottish physicist James Clerk Maxwell obtains the first color photograph by using light filters to produce three separate negatives.

1861

Flexible film
The Kodak camera uses a roll of photosensitized celluloid film. The film could be used for 100 photographs using exposures of only a fraction of a second.

1889

Color photograph
The Lumière brothers perfect the procedure of using glass plates covered with different colored grains to produce images formed by tiny points of primary colors.

1907

The video photograph
Sony produces a reflex camera that records images on a magnetic disc. The images could be viewed on a television set.

1989

Video

C reated at the end of the 1950s, video was originally a technology linked to television. Before its invention, programs had to be broadcast live, with all of the inconveniences associated with such a live event. Very soon, new possibilities were found for video, and in 1965, the Korean artist Nam June Paik made the first art video. In 1968, Sony developed the first portable video camera. On the other hand, the launch of the VCR system by Philips in 1970 made viewing movies at home a part of everyday life. ●

Manual focus ring

Lens

1. IMAGE RECORDER
Digital cameras allow for capturing video as well as for taking pictures, using the same technology.

CCD chip
The image is formed on this sensor by the light that passes through the lens, and the image is transformed by the sensor into electric signals.

Light source

Lens

An internal program translates the light data (analog information) into the binary system (digital information).

The image will be comprised of cells called **pixels.** It can be used directly in a computer.

A built-in microphone allows for the inclusion of high-quality audio.

RECHARGEABLE BATTERY
Up to six hours

LCD ROTATING SCREEN
is used as a monitor or viewfinder. It can be rotated to different angles.

From Analog to Digital Technology

SUPER 8
Eastman Kodak developed an 8 mm-wide film inside a plastic cartridge. The film was used with a portable camera and a projector, and the format was very popular for home movies.
Duration 3 minutes

BETAMAX
Sony developed magnetic tapes that were of high quality but had little recording time. It continued to be manufactured for high-quality recordings until 2002.
Duration 60 minutes

VHS
The Video Home System was developed by JVC. Its advantages included re-recording most movies on a single tape, though some image quality was lost.
Duration 60 to 90 minutes

1965

1975

1976

Several formats

Different systems and media are used for different applications, depending on the final quality desired.

HI8   DIGITAL 8   DVD   **MINI DV**

FOR PROFESSIONAL USE
DV cam
Digital betacam

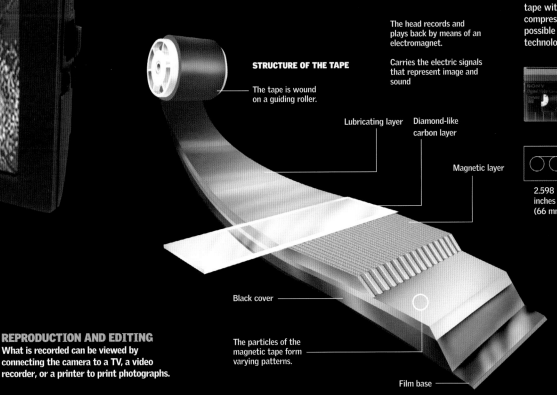

2.
STORAGE
Data is stored as bytes. The image can be reproduced without losing image or audio quality. The level of detail is greater in digital than in analog.

25%
more quality than the analog formats

The head records and plays back by means of an electromagnet.

Carries the electric signals that represent image and sound

STRUCTURE OF THE TAPE

The tape is wound on a guiding roller.

Lubricating layer   Diamond-like carbon layer

Magnetic layer

DIGITAL TAPE
is small, which makes it ideal for portable cameras. Digital tape combines magnetic tape with the data compression made possible by digital technology.

1.889 inches (48 mm)

2.598 inches (66 mm)

Black cover

3.
REPRODUCTION AND EDITING
What is recorded can be viewed by connecting the camera to a TV, a video recorder, or a printer to print photographs.

The particles of the magnetic tape form varying patterns.

Film base

VIDEO 2000
This system of magnetic-tape cassettes used both sides of the tape, similar to audiotape. It was distributed by Philips until 1988.

Duration 8 hours

VHS SYSTEM
The VHS system became a standard for recording and viewing videocassettes. Home viewers and video clubs became popular.

DVD
Philips and Sony introduced this digital disc. It can store every type of digital file, including high-definition video. A laser is used to view it.

Duration of up to 240 minutes

WEBCAMS
These small digital cameras connected to a computer can take photographs and record short videos. Connected to the Internet, they can be used in real time.

1979   1980   1995   2000

Microwaves

T his is the name given to electromagnetic waves found between radio waves and the infrared spectrum. They have many applications, the best known being the microwave oven, developed in 1946 from research conducted by Percy Spencer. Cellular-phone technology, cable TV and Internet, radars, and wireless protocols such as Bluetooth also use microwaves to transfer and receive information. ●

**THE ERS-1 SATELLITE
ORBITING EARTH**
It was launched from the Guyana Space Center in July 1991, and its mission was to map the atmosphere and surface of the Earth by using microwaves.

The Electromagnetic Spectrum

Electromagnetic energy has waves that have specific length and frequency within a continuous range known as the electromagnetic spectrum.

UNITS OF MEASUREMENT

Length of the wave	Meters
Frequency	Hertz

ELECTRIC CURRENT

The frequency is a measure of the number of times that the electromagnetic field oscillates in one second.

The greater the wavelength, the less the energy.

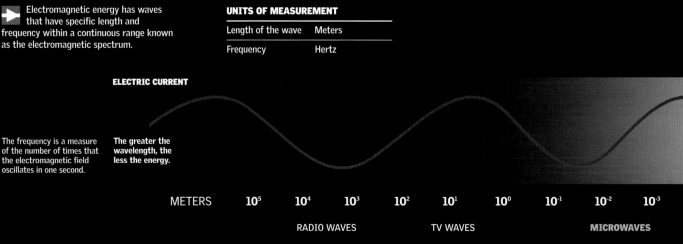

METERS	10^5	10^4	10^3	10^2	10^1	10^0	10^{-1}	10^{-2}	10^{-3}
		RADIO WAVES			TV WAVES			MICROWAVES	

How a Microwave Oven Works

What it does is heat food by using high-frequency electromagnetic waves.

1 Electric plug
Transmits low-frequency electric current

2 Magnetron
The magnetron transforms electric energy into electromagnetic waves (high-frequency microwaves).

3 Microwave oven
The waves are distributed uniformly within the cavity, generating heat by the friction of the molecules present in food and liquids.

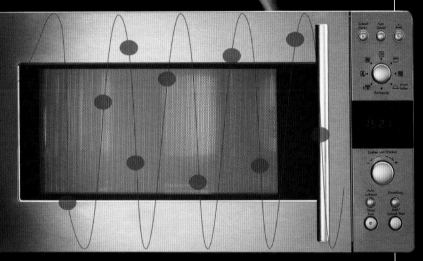

In the winter, we usually rub our hands together to generate heat; this principle is used in microwave ovens.

In Communications

According to the frequency and length of the wave used, the microwaves are also used in radio, TV, and cellular telephones.

CELLULAR TECHNOLOGY
allows communication between users whose locations are unknown or who are mobile. To this end, an infrastructure with base station antennas as its sole visible element must be set up.

1 Radio control
controls and assigns the functions related to radio waves. The geographic area in which the service is rendered is called the coverage area.

2 Base station
The station contains radio equipment that issues electromagnetic waves from communication antennas.

3 Cells and telephones
Each cell has a transmitting base station, which has multiple channels for the simultaneous use of dozens of phones. When a user passes from one cell to another, the phone leaves the frequency it was using and takes an available frequency in the new cell.

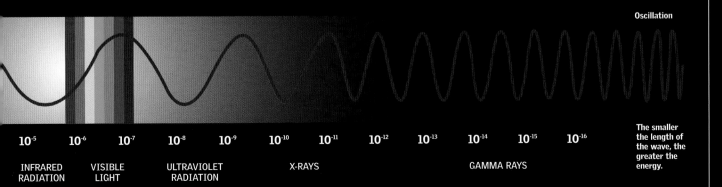

Oscillation

| 10^{-5} | 10^{-6} | 10^{-7} | 10^{-8} | 10^{-9} | 10^{-10} | 10^{-11} | 10^{-12} | 10^{-13} | 10^{-14} | 10^{-15} | 10^{-16} |

INFRARED RADIATION   VISIBLE LIGHT   ULTRAVIOLET RADIATION   X-RAYS   GAMMA RAYS

The smaller the length of the wave, the greater the energy.

Scanners

Several technologies that digitize, read, detect, and trace images, objects, or signals can be grouped under this term. The better known are computer scanners and bar-code scanners, but scanners are also used in medicine, biometric identification, security systems, and detection of radio frequencies. Some computer scanners incorporate text-recognition software, which can digitize printed, typed, or even handwritten text. This capability has been very useful in digitizing a great amount of material at universities and libraries; however, it has also encouraged pirating in publishing. ●

How an Image Is Digitized

The scanner comes from the phrase "to scan." An image is scanned by a head that transforms it into digital data.

It is placed facedown on the transparent screen.

The cover can be removed to scan originals that are very thick.

1. THE ORIGINAL
can be any document with a flat surface, such as a photograph, a paper document, or a page in a book.

LUZ

2. SCANNER HEAD
analyzes a photograph and converts it into digital information.

LINE BY LINE
The scanner head reads one small horizontal strip at a time.

Once a strip is finished, the head moves and reads the following one.

Each strip can be less than 0.00039 inch (0.01 mm) thick.

HOW IT WORKS

1 Light bounces against the original and takes on its colors.

2 A system of mirrors and lenses concentrates this light in the optic sensor.

3 The optic sensor transforms the received light into electric impulses. These are then digitized (transformed into data).

Original

Light source

Lens

Mirrors

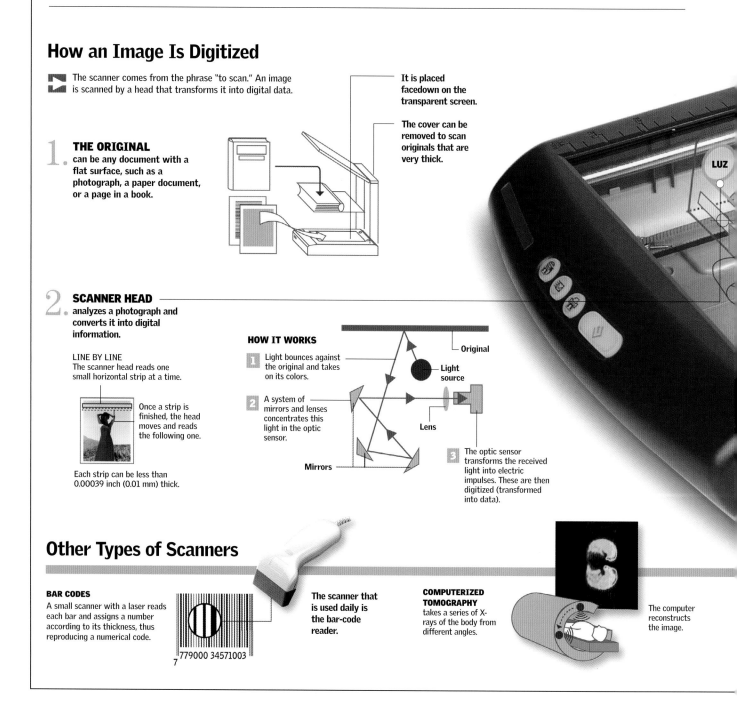

Other Types of Scanners

BAR CODES
A small scanner with a laser reads each bar and assigns a number according to its thickness, thus reproducing a numerical code.

779000 34571003
7

The scanner that is used daily is the bar-code reader.

COMPUTERIZED TOMOGRAPHY
takes a series of X-rays of the body from different angles.

The computer reconstructs the image.

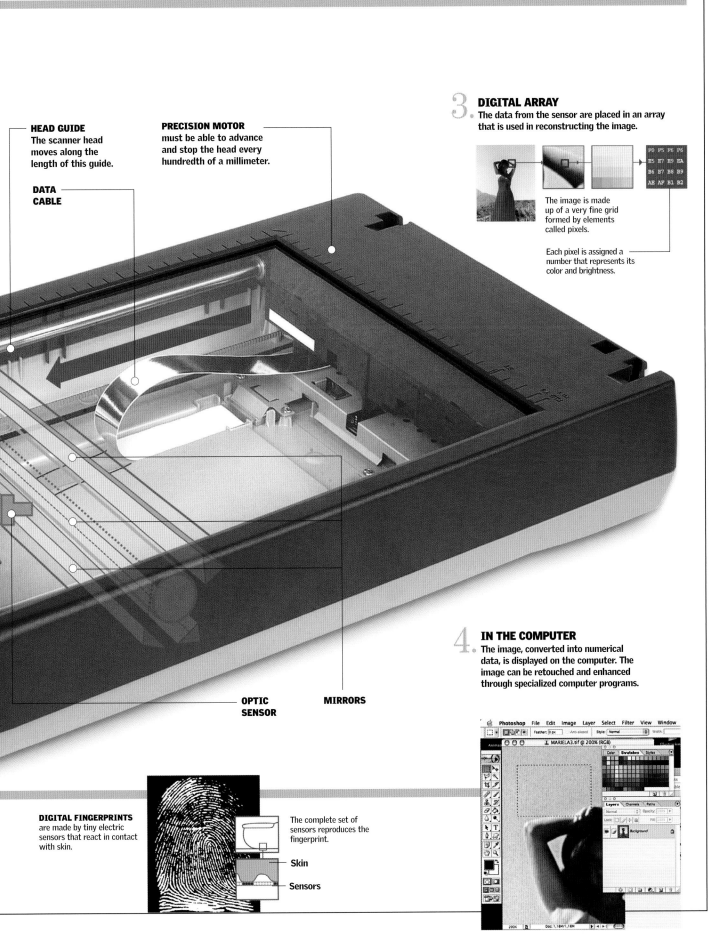

HEAD GUIDE
The scanner head moves along the length of this guide.

DATA CABLE

PRECISION MOTOR
must be able to advance and stop the head every hundredth of a millimeter.

3. DIGITAL ARRAY
The data from the sensor are placed in an array that is used in reconstructing the image.

F0	F5	F6	F6
E5	E7	E9	EA
B6	B7	B8	B9
AE	AF	B1	B2

The image is made up of a very fine grid formed by elements called pixels.

Each pixel is assigned a number that represents its color and brightness.

OPTIC SENSOR

MIRRORS

4. IN THE COMPUTER
The image, converted into numerical data, is displayed on the computer. The image can be retouched and enhanced through specialized computer programs.

DIGITAL FINGERPRINTS
are made by tiny electric sensors that react in contact with skin.

The complete set of sensors reproduces the fingerprint.

— **Skin**

— **Sensors**

Athletic Shoes

These shoes were already used in ancient times in Mesopotamia and Egypt, but they became widely used in the last decades of the 20th century. The first athletic shoes appeared in 1893. They were made of canvas and were used so that sailors did not need to walk with shoes along the docks. Today athletic shoes incorporate true technological advances designed to meet the needs of each sport. For instance, athletic shoes have begun to incorporate air chambers, located between the insole and the external covering of the sole that act as cushions to protect the foot.

13 ounces (390 g)
IS THE WEIGHT OF THIS ATHLETIC SHOE.

SIDE PANELS
For ventilation

METALLIC MESH
Ultrathin to ward off dust

HIGHLY ENGINEERED MESH
allows air but not dirt to pass through.

TOE CAP
provides a good fit and molds to the foot. Depending on the sport, it offers protection or low weight and breathability.

Interior

Many different materials are used. Models for running must satisfy requirements for cushioning, stability, and ventilation.

COUNTER
Made of a semirigid material, the reinforcement covers the heel internally and can prevent instability.

INSOLE
reduces excess heat and friction. Made of foam rubber or EVA to provide extra cushioning.

LATERAL MOVEMENT
is one of the most dangerous movements for sports people. A good shoe controls the natural movement of the foot. There are three types of footstep.

SUPINATION
needs flexible shoes and cushioning.
2 percent of the population

NEUTRAL
Correct and without any disorders
24 percent of the population

PRONATION
leans toward the inside because of a person being flat-footed or overweight.
74 percent of the population

CUSHIONING SYSTEM
Viscous cushioning material, placed in the area of impact for running

MIDSOLE
joins the front toe cap (to which it is sewn) with the insole (to which it is glued).

FASTENING SYSTEM
Shoelaces, zippers, or Velcro. They must fasten the shoe in such a way that the foot can flex in movement.

CHASSIS
Used for reinforcement The openings provide airflow.

INNER SOLE
Their function is to provide comfort and stability and to support the foot. They must be light and flexible.

RUNNING

SOCCER

BASKETBALL

TENNIS

HIKING

CROSS TRAINING

RUGBY

HANDBALL

TOE GUARD
Protection from rubbing against the toe cap

SOLE
can be made of solid or natural rubber. Some include air bubbles that compress when impacted. Each sport requires a different design whose main function is to provide a good grip on the surface.

Grip

Flexibility

Track shoes include nails, and soccer shoes include cleats that can sink into the soil for a better grip.

Biomechanics of Racing

1 IMPACT
When running, the movement of the foot is cyclic. It requires the cushioning of the heel, the part of the foot that undergoes repeated impact.

The heel hits the ground with a force three to four times the weight of the body.

2 LANDING
With support, the foot naturally rotates inward (pronation). The stabilizing elements prevent excessive pronation.

3 IMPULSE
The pressure shifts from the heel to the front of the foot, which is compressed as it pushes off the ground.

Breakthrough Inventions

In the history of technology, there are milestone inventions that radically changed the world and the way we perceive it. Many of these inventions, such as cinematography or the radio, are the realization of the longtime hopes and dreams of humankind. Others, such as the Internet, the cellular telephone, or GPS, have transformed the way we communicate and have

dramatically shortened distances between people. Inventions such as the printing press and the computer chip led to the dramatic development of the arts and sciences, enabling in turn the appearance of more new technologies. Others, such as computers, have not only become indispensable tools, but they have also led us to question the nature of intelligence. ●

Skyscrapers

The development of new materials—especially high-performance concrete and steel—has led to the design and construction of buildings to heights never achieved before. For architects and engineers who work on the construction of large skyscrapers, the greatest challenges lie in ensuring the adequate delivery of services, from elevator systems and gas and water lines to complex emergency systems. There is also a new issue to deal with: how to make the structures less vulnerable to potential terrorist attacks, especially after the September 11, 2001, attacks in New York City. ●

From the Ground to the Sky

The construction of a skyscraper begins with the digging of a large pit for the foundation that will support the entire edifice. This structure of concrete and steel has to take into consideration the weight of the building, lateral resistance to winds, and, possibly, earthquakes.

1 The steel and concrete foundation is made up of a series of bases. Each base supports one of the main columns.

The core
provides the skyscraper with strong lateral resistance. It is also made of concrete and steel and generally houses service elements (elevators, stairways, etc.).

2 The weight of the building rests upon columns made of high-performance, reinforced concrete.

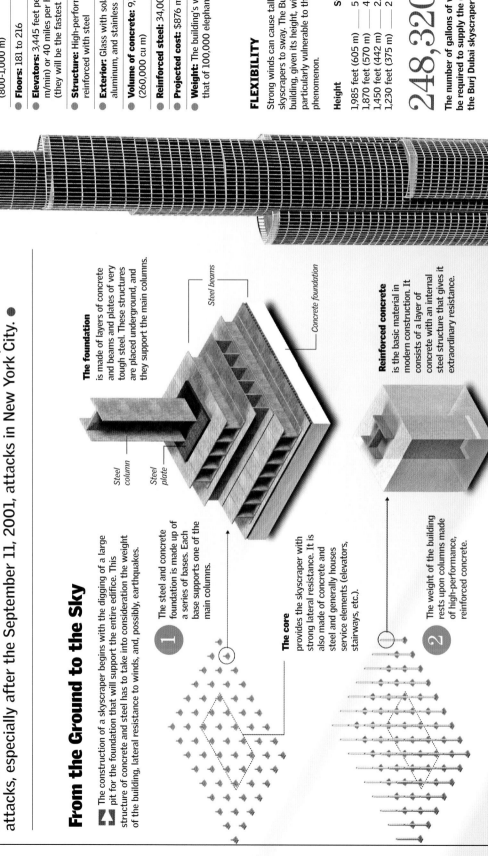

The foundation
is made of layers of concrete and beams and plates of very tough steel. These structures are placed underground, and they support the main columns.

Steel beams

Concrete foundation

Steel column

Steel plate

Reinforced concrete
is the basic material in modern construction. It consists of a layer of concrete with an internal steel structure that gives it extraordinary resistance.

The Burj Dubai

Is the tallest building in the world and is currently under construction in Dubai, United Arab Emirates. Its final height has been kept secret to avoid potential competition, but it is believed that it will be anywhere from 2,625 to 3,280 feet (800–1,000 m).

TECHNICAL SPECIFICATIONS

- **Height:** Between 2,625 and 3,280 feet (800–1,000 m)
- **Floors:** 181 to 216
- **Elevators:** 3,445 feet per minute (1,050 m/min) or 40 miles per hour (65 km/h) (they will be the fastest in the world)
- **Structure:** High-performance concrete reinforced with steel
- **Exterior:** Glass with solar filters, aluminum, and stainless steel
- **Volume of concrete:** 9,181,810 cubic feet (260,000 cu m)
- **Reinforced steel:** 34,000 tons
- **Projected cost:** $876 million
- **Weight:** The building's weight will equal that of 100,000 elephants.

FLEXIBILITY

Strong winds can cause tall skyscrapers to sway. The Burj Dubai building, given its height, will be particularly vulnerable to this phenomenon.

Height	Sway
1,985 feet (605 m)	5 feet (1.5 m)
1,870 feet (570 m)	4 feet (1.25 m)
1,450 feet (442 m)	2.5 feet (.75 m)
1,230 feet (375 m)	2 feet (.5 m)

248,320

The number of gallons of water that will be required to supply the daily demand at the Burj Dubai skyscraper

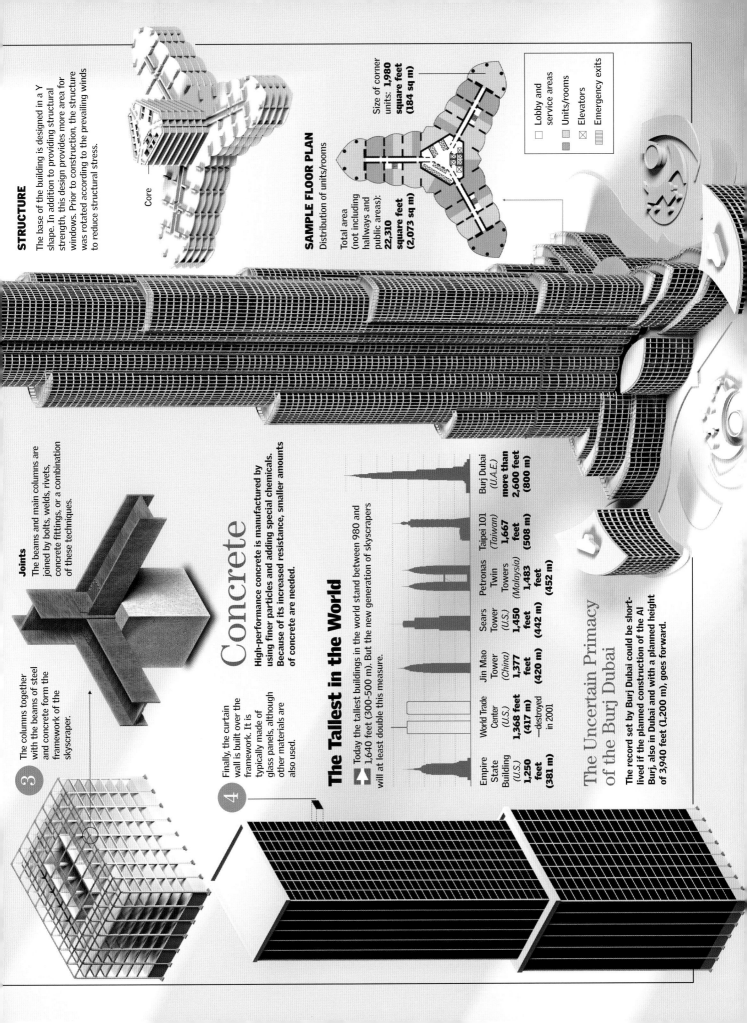

STRUCTURE

The base of the building is designed in a Y shape. In addition to providing structural strength, this design provides more area for windows. Prior to construction, the structure was rotated according to the prevailing winds to reduce structural stress.

Core

SAMPLE FLOOR PLAN
Distribution of units/rooms

Size of corner units: **1,980 square feet (184 sq m)**

Total area (not including hallways and public areas): **22,310 square feet (2,073 sq m)**

- ☐ Lobby and service areas
- ▨ Units/rooms
- ⊠ Elevators
- ▥ Emergency exits

Joints

The beams and main columns are joined by bolts, welds, rivets, concrete fittings, or a combination of these techniques.

③ The columns together with the beams of steel and concrete form the framework of the skyscraper.

Concrete

High-performance concrete is manufactured by using finer particles and adding special chemicals. Because of its increased resistance, smaller amounts of concrete are needed.

④ Finally, the curtain wall is built over the framework. It is typically made of glass panels, although other materials are also used.

The Tallest in the World

Today the tallest buildings in the world stand between 980 and 1,640 feet (300-500 m). But the new generation of skyscrapers will at least double this measure.

Empire State Building (U.S.)	World Trade Center (U.S.)	Jin Mao Tower (China)	Sears Tower (U.S.)	Petronas Twin Towers (Malaysia)	Taipei 101 (Taiwan)	Burj Dubai (U.A.E.)
1,250 feet (381 m)	1,368 feet (417 m) —destroyed in 2001	1,377 feet (420 m)	1,450 feet (442 m)	1,483 feet (452 m)	1,667 feet (508 m)	more than 2,600 feet (800 m)

The Uncertain Primacy of the Burj Dubai

The record set by Burj Dubai could be short-lived if the planned construction of the Al Burj, also in Dubai and with a planned height of 3,940 feet (1,200 m), goes forward.

The Cellular Telephone

Few inventions have had as widespread an impact as the cellular phone. In just two-and-a-half decades, the cellular phone has become extremely popular around the world and almost indispensable for populations in the developed world, to the point that sales already surpass one billion units a year. The latest cell phones, in addition to being small, portable, and light, are true workstations that far exceed their original function of keeping the user connected at any time and place.

Communication

Providers divide an area into a system of cell sites. Each site has an antenna that detects the presence of a particular cell phone in its area and identifies it through the phone's unique code.

1 Calling

When a number is dialed, the antenna at the local cell site identifies the caller and the called party. It then transmits this information to the switch.

2 The switch

The switch maintains a database of all the cell phones that are turned on and their cell-site locations. It then locates the position of the called party and sends the information to the appropriate cell site.

28 ounces (780 g)

is the weight of the Motorola DynaTAC 8000X, which was the first commercially available cellular phone. More recent models weigh less than 2 ounces (50 g).

The Evolution of the Cell Phone

Since the first cell phone appeared on the market in 1983, mobile telephones have become smaller and, at the same time, they have incorporated dozens of new features, such as Internet connectivity, picture taking, and videoconferencing; the mobile telephones also play music.

1983	1993	1996	1999	1999	2000	2001
Motorola DynaTAC 8000X	**Simon Personal Communicator**	**Motorola StarTAC**	**Nokia 7110**	**Sharp J-SH04**	**Samsung SCH-M105**	**Kyocera QCP6035**
First cellular phone	First PDA/cell phone Added applications such as a calculator, calendar, address book, etc.	First clamshell cell phone Design reaches the cell phone	One of the first to use Wireless Application Protocol (WAP)	First cell-phone camera (released only in Japan)	First MP3 cell phone	First Palm-powered cell phone

In Motion

▶ Cell sites detect the movement of a cell phone; as the signal weakens at one site, it becomes stronger at another. This movement allows seamless communication, even during high-speed movement from one cell site to another.

When a cell phone user moves away from the service provider's network, the service can be provided by another carrier. The phone is then in roaming mode.

INTERNATIONAL CALLS

As is the case with landline phones, international communications are facilitated with the assistance of satellites.

Smartphones

▶ In addition to being a telephone and having such traditional features as a calendar, calculator, and camera, a smartphone incorporates advanced computing capabilities for connecting to the Internet through Wi-Fi and to other devices through Bluetooth.

③ **Connecting**
The local cell-site antenna establishes communication with the requested cell phone.

3 billion

is the approximate number of cell phone subscribers in the world, according to the latest data. This number is equal to almost half of the world population.

BlackBerry

12:21 PM   WED, MAY 25   EDGE

3 ▢

(3) Messages

2001	2005	2007
Panasonic P2101V	**Motorola ROKR**	**iPhone**
Among the first third-generation cell phones (with videoconferencing)	First cell phone with iTunes	has a 3.5-inch (8.9-cm) touch screen and Wi-Fi Web access.

GPS

The Global Positioning System (GPS) allows a person to locate his or her position anywhere on the planet, at any time, using a small handheld receiver. Originally developed as a military project, GPS has now reached every corner of civilian life. Today it is not only an essential tool in ships and aircraft, but it is also becoming, due to its multiple applications, a common feature in vehicles as well as in athletic and scientific equipment. ●

Features

 Since GPS is a dynamic system, it also provides real-time data about the movement, direction, and speed of the user, allowing for a myriad of uses.

1 **Location**
The civilian user determines his or her position using three-dimensional geographic coordinates, with a margin of error between 7 and 50 feet (2-15 m) depending on the quality of the receiver and the satellites it detects at any given moment.

2 **Maps**
Extrapolation of the coordinates using geographic charts of cities, roads, rivers, oceans, and airspace can produce a dynamic map of the user's position and movement.

3 **Tracking**
The user can know the speed at which he or she is traveling, the distance traveled, and the time elapsed. In addition, other information is provided, such as average speed.

4 **Trips**
Trips can be programmed using predetermined points (waypoints). During the trip, the GPS receiver provides information about the remaining distance to each waypoint, the correct direction, and the estimated time of arrival.

Icon and name of the next waypoint (in this case, an exit)

Distance to the next waypoint

Time elapsed

Direction to the next waypoint

Speed

APPLICATIONS

Although it was originally developed as a navigational system, GPS is used today in a variety of fields. The free use of this tool for work, business, recreation, and sports activities is changing the way we move and act.

SPORTS
GPS devices keep the athlete informed on time, speed, and distance.

MILITARY
Used in remote-controlled and navigational systems

SCIENTIFIC
Used in paleontology, archaeology, and animal tracking

EXPLORATION
Provides orientation and marks reference points

TRANSPORTATION
Air and maritime navigation. Its use is growing in automobiles.

AGRICULTURE
Maps areas of greater or lesser fertility within different plots of land

Satellites, Lighthouses in the Sky

The Navstar GPS satellites are the heart of the system. The satellites emit signals that are interpreted by the GPS receiver to determine its location on a map. The system has a constellation of 24 main satellites that orbit the Earth at an altitude of 12,550 miles (20,200 km), collectively covering the entire surface of the planet. They circle the Earth every 12 hours.

1 The receiver detects one of the satellites and calculates its distance. This distance is the radius of a sphere whose center is the satellite and on whose surface the user can be located, although at a point yet to be determined.

2 When a second satellite is detected and the distance calculated, a second sphere is formed that intersects with the first sphere along a circle. The user can be located anywhere along the perimeter of this circle.

3 A third satellite forms a third sphere that intersects the circle at two points. One of the points is ruled out as an invalid location (for example, a position above the surface of the Earth). The other point is the correct location. The more satellites used, the lower the margin of error.

Clocks

Thanks to data received from the satellites, civilian GPS receivers also function as atomic clocks (the most precise in the world), although several thousands of dollars cheaper.

CALCULATING DISTANCES

Once the GPS satellites are detected by the GPS receiver, the receiver's challenge is to precisely calculate its distance and position in relation to those satellites.

1 The receiver has in its memory the satellites' ephemerides (from the Greek word *ephemeros*, meaning "daily")—that is, their position in the sky by the hour and day.

2 Upon detection of a satellite, it receives a highly complex signal of on-off pulses called a pseudo-random code.

Each satellite has its own code that helps the receiver identify it. The code travels at the speed of light.

Satellite code

3 The receiver recognizes the code and the exact time of each repetition (the signal includes corrections to the receiver's clock). By means of comparison, the receiver determines the lag in the satellite's signal, and since it knows the signal's speed, it can determine the distance.

Satellite code

Receiver code

Lag

750 The annual cost, in millions of dollars, to maintain the entire Global Positioning System.

The Computer Chip

Without this small electronic device, the majority of new technologies from the past few years would not exist. The computer chip is present in myriad objects used every day. Despite its limited dimensions, each chip contains thousands or millions of interconnected electronic devices (mainly diodes and transistors) and also passive components (such as resistors and capacitors). Its invention was made possible with the discovery that semiconductor elements could accomplish the same functions as vacuum tubes but with a much superior performance and at considerably lower cost. •

What It Is

▶ It is a thin silicon wafer that measures less than half an inch (1.3 cm) across and can contain several million electronic components.

0.02 inch
(0.6 mm)

is the size of the smallest computer chip in the world. It is used to detect counterfeit bills.

SOME APPLICATIONS

HOME	Microwave ovens, digital clocks
OFFICE	Computers, calculators
COMMUNICATIONS	Telephones, TV, radio
TRANSPORTATION	Air and land traffic control
MEDICINE	Diagnostic equipment
ENTERTAINMENT	Audio, video games
MILITARY	Weapons

SIZE REDUCTION

Continuing improvements in the techniques of computer-chip fabrication have allowed the development of ever-tinier electronic components.

TRADITIONAL TRANSISTOR
Simple capsule

0.2 inch (5 mm)

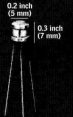

0.3 inch (7 mm)

CHIP
can contain millions of transistors.

0.5 inch (1.3 cm)

0.5 inch (1.3 cm)
ACTUAL SIZE

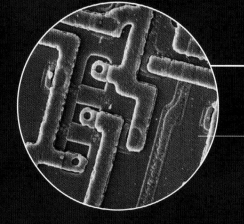

TRANSISTOR
Etched in the silicon, the transistor is a very effective semiconductor device and amplifier, but microscopic in size. The smallest ones measure 50 nanometers.

HOW TRANSISTORS WORK

Transistors act like electronic switches that are activated and deactivated by means of an electrical signal.

ACTIVE CIRCUIT

1 The **negatively charged** (doped) silicon has atoms with free electrons.

3 An electrical signal is applied.

Negative silicon

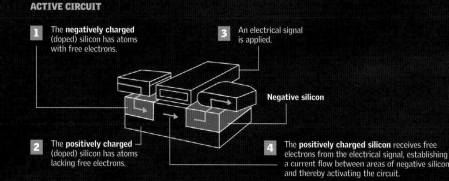

2 The **positively charged** (doped) silicon has atoms lacking free electrons.

4 The **positively charged silicon** receives free electrons from the electrical signal, establishing a current flow between areas of negative silicon and thereby activating the circuit.

INACTIVE CIRCUIT

5 The electrical signal is interrupted.

6 The current does not flow, and the circuit is deactivated.

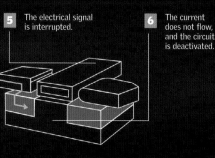

Where They Are Found

PRINTED CIRCUIT BOARDS
are used inside electronic
devices. They are tiny and
placed on top of a copper
sheet that is laminated
onto a plastic board.

INTEGRATED CIRCUITS
are mounted on printed
circuit boards and are
connected via copper
pathways.

contain the
computer **chip**

**COPPER
PATHWAYS**

PACKAGE
Plastic or
ceramic casing

PINS
are small metallic legs
that connect the
integrated circuit to
the printed circuit.

CHIP
A layered silicon
wafer that contains
electronic
components

GOLD WIRES
are soldered to chip
terminals and connect
them to the pins.

THE INVENTOR
Jack Kilby developed the
first integrated circuit in
1959. His invention had a
huge impact on the
development of the
electronics industry.

Jack Kilby
Electrical engineer from
the United States. He was
awarded the Nobel Prize
for Physics in 2000.

Evolution of the
Computer Chip

YEAR	MODEL	TRANSISTORS
1971	4004	2,250
1978	8086	29,000
1985	386	275,000
1989	486	1,180,000
1993	PENTIUM	3,100,000
2000	PENTIUM 4	42,000,000

First Integrated Circuit

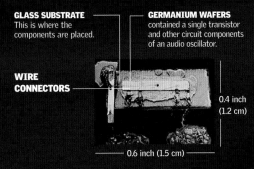

GLASS SUBSTRATE
This is where the
components are placed.

GERMANIUM WAFERS
contained a single transistor
and other circuit components
of an audio oscillator.

**WIRE
CONNECTORS**

0.4 inch
(1.2 cm)

0.6 inch (1.5 cm)

The Computer

From the huge calculating machines that occupied entire rooms to today's home and laptop models, computers have revolutionized how we see the world and relate to it. Today our everyday lives are characterized by information technology, whether for recreation, work, study, or communication. Already under development are quantum computers and so-called molecular computers, which are biocomputers that use DNA as the basis of their circuits and that have the ability to replicate themselves. ●

LAPTOP MODELS
have a rechargeable battery and smaller dimensions. They basically have the same features as a PC.

The Personal Computer

is made up of various interconnected devices (the hardware) and programs (the software). The core is a very powerful microprocessor that contains all the devices and is installed on the motherboard.

PROGRAM
is the component most closely related to the user. It is also known as application software. It allows the user to accomplish tasks, such as processing text and images, performing calculations, managing databases, and using the Internet.

MONITOR
The images are formed by tiny cells called pixels, which use the additive primary colors red, green, and blue. High-resolution monitors can have an array of up to 1,920 x 1,200 pixels.

OPERATING SYSTEM
Windows is the one most commonly used. It presents the system in a user-friendly way, using icons, folders, and windows.

ACCESS DEVICES

Key

Conducting surface

Printed circuit

KEYBOARD
It is used to enter data (numbers, letters, and symbols) by sending coded signals to the microprocessor. When a key is pressed, a contact is closed.

UNDERSIDE

A video camera registers movement.

A light-emitting diode (LED) illuminates the surface beneath it.

OPTICAL MOUSE
controls the placement of the cursor in the computer's graphic interface. It registers any movement of the mouse and calculates the coordinates of the movement.

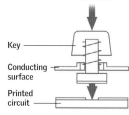

STORAGE DEVICES
are used to save information or transport information to another computer.

CD/DVD READER/RECORDER
reads and also records CDs and DVDs.

HARD DISK
saves programs and folders as permanent, magnetically recorded data.

FLOPPY DRIVE
reads and records information on flexible floppy disks (diskettes).

COMPUTER TOWER
is the case that holds the main components.

CONNECTORS
are used to connect peripheral devices, such as a modem, scanner, or printer.

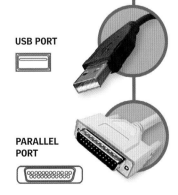

USB PORT

PARALLEL PORT

How a Computer Works

Example of the routing of information during a basic process

1 INPUT
Data enters the computer through a keyboard, mouse, or modem and is interpreted by the appropriate circuit.

2 MICROPROCESSOR
controls all computer functions. It processes the entered data and carries out the necessary arithmetic and logic calculations.

3 RAM MEMORY
temporarily stores all the information and programs used by the microprocessor.

4 PROCESSING
Data can travel back and forth from the CPU to the RAM several times until processing is complete.

5 STORAGE
Data is sent to a storage device (for example, the hard disk).

6 OUTPUT
The information on the monitor is updated through the video card.

Essential Components

MOTHERBOARD
The main printed circuit board to which all other hardware components are connected

ROM MEMORY
(Read Only Memory)
Used to store the basic startup instructions for the computer

EXPANSION SLOTS
allow for the insertion of circuit boards to incorporate more devices.

The Internet

I s a worldwide network where interconnected computers of every type can exchange information. The social impact of the Internet is comparable to the invention of the printing press, enabling the free flow of information and access to it from anywhere in the world. With the appearance of blogs, the world of editing and journalism has become democratic, since virtually anyone can publish their own texts, images, and opinions.

HOW IT IS SET UP

The Internet is a worldwide network in which one participates through a service provider, which receives, saves, and distributes information using its computer "server." The user's computer connects to the Internet using a variety of methods, programs, and devices.

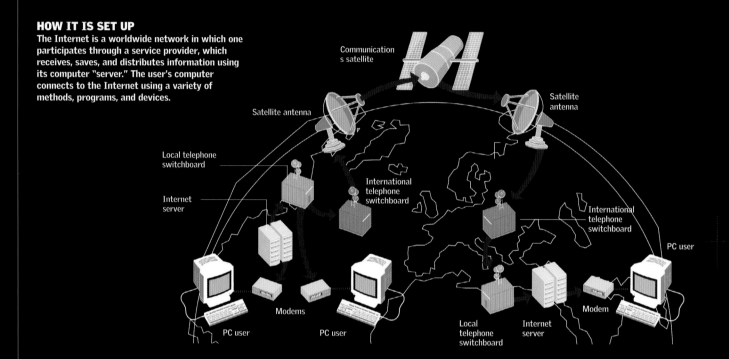

Communications satellite

Satellite antenna

Satellite antenna

Local telephone switchboard

Internet server

International telephone switchboard

International telephone switchboard

PC user

Modems

Modem

PC user

PC user

Local telephone switchboard

Internet server

THE BROWSER

is a program that allows the user to see documents on the World Wide Web and to go from one document to another using the hypertext transfer protocol (HTTP). The most common browsers are Internet Explorer, Netscape, and Firefox.

A WEB SITE OR WEB PAGE

contains a series of documents written in hypertext markup language (HTML) combined with other, more sophisticated languages, such as Java and Flash animation.

ELECTRONIC MAIL

travels from one computer to another through e-mail servers. It can carry attachments, such as photos or text documents.

SEARCH ENGINES

are tools used to find information available on the World Wide Web. They function like a database that is constantly being updated by robots that prowl the Web and collect information. The most commonly used search engines are Google and Yahoo; they also offer other services to their users, such as e-mail and news updates.

CHAT

This service allows a group of users to communicate with each other in real time. It started out only in written form, but it is now possible to transmit audio and video images via webcams.

VOICE OVER IP

is a system that allows a computer to communicate with a regular telephone anywhere in the world, bypassing normal telephone charges. It requires an Internet connection and a program that enables this type of communication.

Transmitting Information

▶ These interconnected systems share information internally and with external users, forming networks. Information travels from one computer to another through such a network.

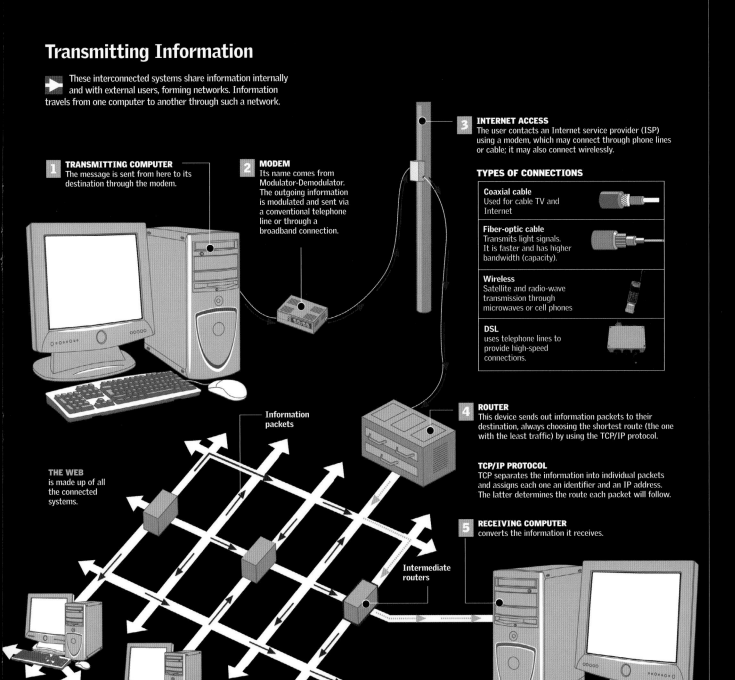

1 TRANSMITTING COMPUTER
The message is sent from here to its destination through the modem.

2 MODEM
Its name comes from Modulator-Demodulator. The outgoing information is modulated and sent via a conventional telephone line or through a broadband connection.

3 INTERNET ACCESS
The user contacts an Internet service provider (ISP) using a modem, which may connect through phone lines or cable; it may also connect wirelessly.

TYPES OF CONNECTIONS

Coaxial cable
Used for cable TV and Internet

Fiber-optic cable
Transmits light signals. It is faster and has higher bandwidth (capacity).

Wireless
Satellite and radio-wave transmission through microwaves or cell phones

DSL
uses telephone lines to provide high-speed connections.

Information packets

THE WEB
is made up of all the connected systems.

4 ROUTER
This device sends out information packets to their destination, always choosing the shortest route (the one with the least traffic) by using the TCP/IP protocol.

TCP/IP PROTOCOL
TCP separates the information into individual packets and assigns each one an identifier and an IP address. The latter determines the route each packet will follow.

5 RECEIVING COMPUTER
converts the information it receives.

Intermediate routers

Cinematography

Since the middle of the 19th century, the desire to produce moving images has resulted in the development of a large variety of mechanical devices, such as the praxinoscope and the zoetrope. The appearance of celluloid film allowed real images to be captured to show movement. The introduction of sound was a revolutionary innovation, even more so than the introduction of color. The idea of three-dimensional images has also been pursued, with mixed results. Today IMAX technology allows viewers to become immersed in the film they are watching. ●

IMAX Technology

▶ is the most advanced motion-picture projection system. Invented in Canada, it is used in more than 228 movie theaters across North America and Europe. As of today, only four theaters have all three projection systems: IMAX, Omnimax, and IMAX 3-D.

Omnimax

THE SCREEN
is metallic, hemispherical, and white. It wraps over the seats like a dome. It takes four minutes just to open it.

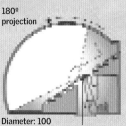

180º
projection

Diameter: 100
feet (30 m)

Projector

Varieties

IMAX 3-D
Viewers must wear glasses that allow them to see in three dimensions.

FLAT IMAX
uses a silver-colored flat screen, which reflects projected light more strongly than a white screen.

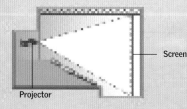

Projector

Screen

SOUND
27,000 watts of power
Sound passes through small holes in the screen and travels throughout the whole theater.

SEATS
The seats recline and the viewer cannot see the edge of the screen, creating the feeling of being immersed in the movie.

THE PROJECTOR
The system provides greater image stability.

FRAMES
are 10 times larger than a traditional motion-picture frame, providing better image definition.

IMAX
frame

Traditional
35-mm
frame

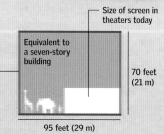

Size of screen in
theaters today

Equivalent to
a seven-story
building

Screen

70 feet
(21 m)

95 feet (29 m)

MOVIE SET
French director, screenwriter, and actress Nicole Garcia on the set of her movie *Every Other Weekend (Un Week-end sur deux)*.

The First Projection Systems

1400

Roger Bacon invents the magic lantern, the first step toward the modern projector.

Objective lens

Light beam

Projected image

Image support

The light source was an oil lamp

1895

The Lumière brothers invent the first projector, inspired by a sewing machine, and hold a screening in Paris.

Crank for advancing the film strip through the projector

Object lens: expanded the film frame up to 35 x 24 inches (90 x 60 cm).

Wheels supported the film strip and helped advance it

1932

Color movies appear. The Technicolor camera superimposes three films—red, blue, and green—to produce a color image.

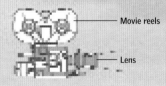

Movie reels

Lens

Television

T he origins of television date back to 1884, when Paul Nipkow invented a rotating scanning disk camera for capturing moving images, but it was only in 1936 when the first modern TV broadcast was made in England. The invention of radar during World War II reduced the costs of this technology, making it accessible to the general public. In spite of its slow beginning, television became an important medium for communication, greatly influencing the opinions, behaviors, and imagination of several generations. Today analog technology is being replaced by digital technology, and three-dimensional television is at the experimental stage. ●

1. TAPING
The camera captures images through its lens and sound through a microphone.

A VIDEO
The image is divided into a series of horizontal lines.

Each line is made up of points of different brightness. By convention, they are split into the three primary colors: red, green, and blue.

B SOUND
is codified and broadcast using the same method as the one employed in FM radio.

2. TRANSMISSION
Images and sound are transmitted together through radio, coaxial cable, or fiber-optic cable.
Each frequency is split between the image (AM) and the sound (FM).

VIA SATELLITE
Uses high-frequency radio waves. The signal can cover an entire country.

VIA AIRWAVES
Employs a system similar to AM and FM radio

VIA CABLE
A coaxial or fiber-optic cable permits the reception of a large number of channels.

3. RECEPTION
RECONSTRUCTING MOVEMENT

 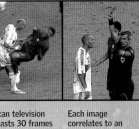

Each image is like a still photograph of a single moment.

American television broadcasts 30 frames per second at 60 hertz (60 times per second), while European television broadcasts 25 frames per second at 50 hertz.

Each image correlates to an instant in time.

The images are integrated in the brain, resulting in the illusion of continuous movement.

RECONSTRUCTING THE IMAGE

Each image is shown twice. The 30 (25) frames per second are seen as 60 (50) fields per second.

In interlaced-format broadcasts, only half of the display lines of the image are swept with each field. One field delivers the odd-numbered lines, and the next delivers the even-numbered lines, and so on until the entire picture is drawn by interlaced scan.

The Printing Press

he social and cultural impact of the invention of the printing press is comparable to the development of language and the invention of the alphabet. It made possible the establishment of a scientific community, in which knowledge can be communicated with ease. In addition, it made the notion of authorship of a text more meaningful, the book became a popular object, and the dominance of Latin ended, definitively displaced by local tongues. According to some theorists, such as Marshall McLuhan, the press fostered the preeminence of words over the image, changing the way we understand the world today. ◐

Digital Printing Systems

▶ eliminate the need for film (used in traditional printing processes). These machines can accomplish all the steps of production up to delivery of the finished product. The development of the digital printing systems began in the 1990s.

3. PRINTING
Ink is transferred to the paper. The machine is equipped with a rod that flips the paper over for two-sided printing (front and back).

4. CUTTING AND FOLDING
The printed spool of paper is cut, and the sheets are arranged so that the pages line up in proper order, including the cover.

5. BINDING AND FINISHING
The pages are stapled or glued together, and knife blades trim off the excess border to the publication's final size.

2. PAPER ENTRANCE

HEWLETT PACKARD INDIGO PRESS

PAPER ROLL

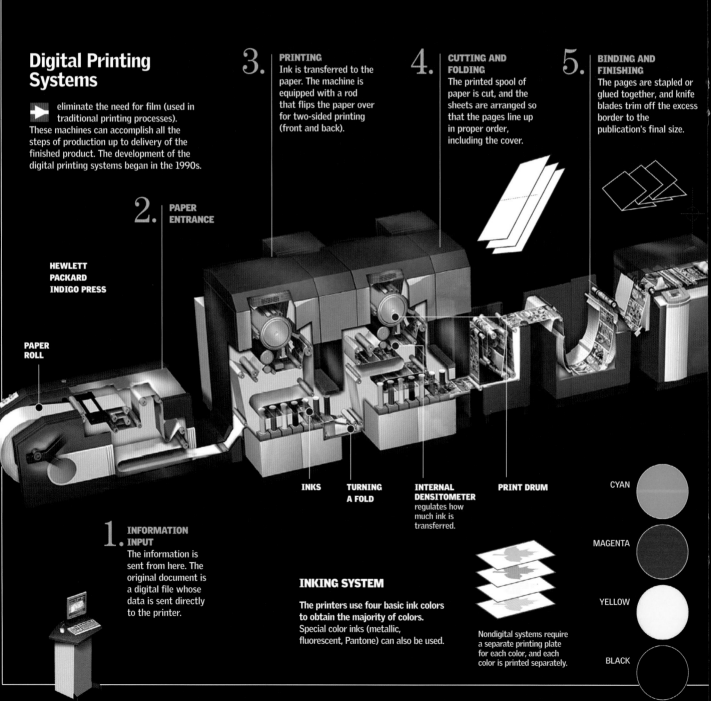

INKS

TURNING A FOLD

INTERNAL DENSITOMETER
regulates how much ink is transferred.

PRINT DRUM

CYAN

MAGENTA

YELLOW

BLACK

1. INFORMATION INPUT
The information is sent from here. The original document is a digital file whose data is sent directly to the printer.

INKING SYSTEM

The printers use four basic ink colors to obtain the majority of colors. Special color inks (metallic, fluorescent, Pantone) can also be used.

Nondigital systems require a separate printing plate for each color, and each color is printed separately.

Different Systems

These processes all require a printing plate or other printing surface but differ in the way they separate the printed area from the nonprinted area.

LETTERPRESS
The printing surface may be rigid or flexible.

FLEXOGRAPHY
The printing surface is flexible.

SERIGRAPHY
The printing surface is a mesh screen.

OFFSET
uses an aluminum printing plate covered with photosensitive material.

ROTOGRAVURE
The printing surface is a copper-coated cylinder with tiny pits, or cells, for the ink.

Technological Advances

In China, multiple copies of an image or text were made by carving wood.

MOVABLE TYPE
Johannes Gutenberg invented a printing system that used metal movable type. Words were assembled letter by letter and could be used to compose different pages.

Metal molds

LITHOGRAPHY
Invented by Alois Senefelder in 1796, lithography is a printing method based on the property of immiscibility of ink and water.

LINOTYPE
is similar to a typewriter. It allowed mechanized typesetting and composition, which until then had been a manual task.

OFFSET
is a printing technique based on lithography that uses plates for the page surface. Currently offset is the most frequently used printing technique.

DIGITAL
Computers eliminate the use of printing plates. Digital printing integrates all production steps in one single machine.

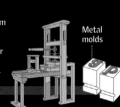

593   Around 1450   1796   1886   1904   1990

The Laser

B ased on quantum mechanics, the laser is an optical device that emits a well-defined photon beam. The result is monochromatic light that can have various properties depending on the purpose for which it is designed. The name is an acronym for Light Amplification by Stimulated Emission of Radiation. When lasers were invented in 1960, they were called a "solution in search of a problem." They have since resolved myriad "problems" in the sciences, the arts, medicine, industry, and everyday life, becoming an essential tool in modern society.

THE INVENTOR
Theodore Maiman

Year	**1960**
Type	**Ruby laser**

It was the first working laser, and it was built using a ruby rod measuring just a few centimeters across.

How a Beam Is Formed

 Light is amplified by stimulated emission of radiation.

1 The ruby rod is shown with its atoms at rest.

2 The light from the lamp stimulates the atoms.

3 Ordinary red light is emitted by the atoms.

Total-reflection mirror

Atoms in the ruby rod

Quartz flash tube

Partially reflecting mirror

The inner surface of the cylinder is polished to reflect the dispersed light.

A few photons escape.

ELECTRIC LIGHT
The amount of light emitted by a small lamp is greater than the amount of light emitted by a laser, but the light does not have a specific wavelength and direction.

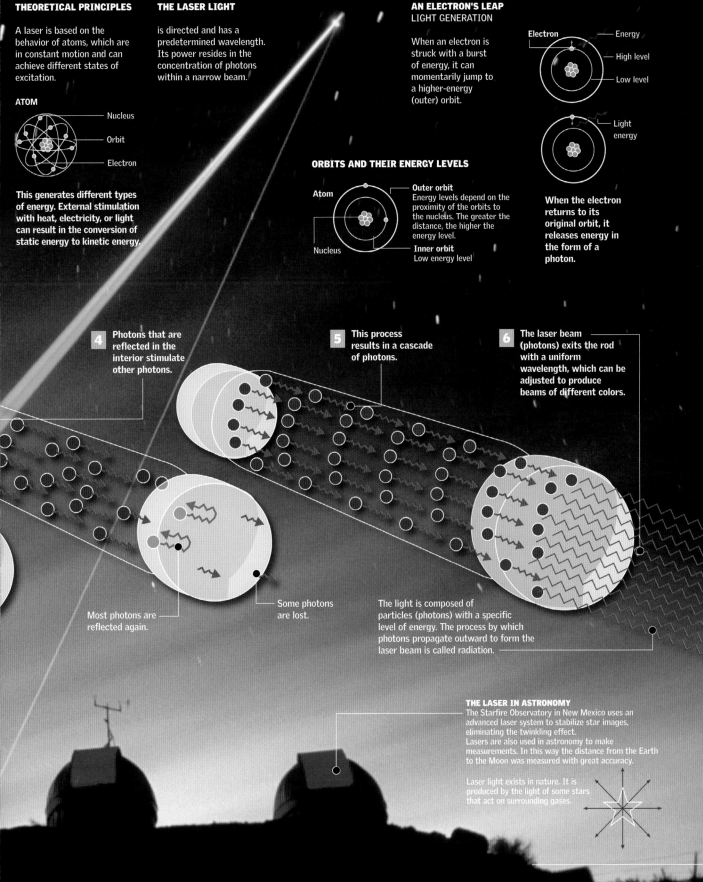

THEORETICAL PRINCIPLES

A laser is based on the behavior of atoms, which are in constant motion and can achieve different states of excitation.

ATOM

- Nucleus
- Orbit
- Electron

This generates different types of energy. External stimulation with heat, electricity, or light can result in the conversion of static energy to kinetic energy.

THE LASER LIGHT

is directed and has a predetermined wavelength. Its power resides in the concentration of photons within a narrow beam.

AN ELECTRON'S LEAP
LIGHT GENERATION

When an electron is struck with a burst of energy, it can momentarily jump to a higher-energy (outer) orbit.

Electron
Energy
High level
Low level

Light energy

When the electron returns to its original orbit, it releases energy in the form of a photon.

ORBITS AND THEIR ENERGY LEVELS

Atom

Outer orbit
Energy levels depend on the proximity of the orbits to the nucleus. The greater the distance, the higher the energy level.

Nucleus

Inner orbit
Low energy level

4 Photons that are reflected in the interior stimulate other photons.

5 This process results in a cascade of photons.

6 The laser beam (photons) exits the rod with a uniform wavelength, which can be adjusted to produce beams of different colors.

Most photons are reflected again.

Some photons are lost.

The light is composed of particles (photons) with a specific level of energy. The process by which photons propagate outward to form the laser beam is called radiation.

THE LASER IN ASTRONOMY

The Starfire Observatory in New Mexico uses an advanced laser system to stabilize star images, eliminating the twinkling effect.
Lasers are also used in astronomy to make measurements. In this way the distance from the Earth to the Moon was measured with great accuracy.

Laser light exists in nature. It is produced by the light of some stars that act on surrounding gases.

Holography

B ased on the optical phenomenon of interference, holography is a photographic technique that allows an image to be recorded in three dimensions on a flat surface. Holograms are often confused with the transmission of three-dimensional images, particularly in science-fiction series and films, such as *Star Trek* or *Star Wars*. Holograms are commonly used as security features on credit cards, currency, and merchandise, because they are difficult to counterfeit. Holography is currently being researched as a way to protect digital data. One of the technologies in development uses high-density crystals to store the data. Another is the so-called Holographic Versatile Disc (HVD). ●

Holographic Recording Process

6,000

is the number of CD-ROMs needed to store the four terabytes contained in an HVD.

1 The laser emits a beam.

2 The beam is split in two.

3 One of the two beams is reflected by a mirror and dispersed by means of a lens, thereby illuminating the object. The second beam is directed at another mirror.

Principles

▶ The creation of holographic images is based on the behavior of light through space, time, and wave interference.

Resulting wave

Wave 2

Wave 1

If two or more wavefronts cross each other, interference is produced. The resulting wave incorporates the positive and negative amplitudes of the original waves.

5 The second beam is reflected by the second mirror, passes through a diverging lens, and illuminates the photosensitive plate.

THE INVENTOR was born in Budapest, Hungary. He received the Nobel Prize for Physics in 1971.

DENNIS GABOR
1900-79

While conducting research to improve the resolution of the electron microscope, Gabor discovered a process that recorded and reproduced three-dimensional images. It was described in 1947, prior to the invention of the laser beam, and became known as holography.

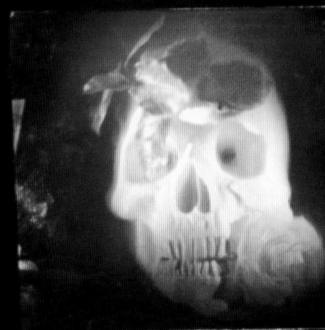

4 A diverging beam illuminates the original object, which reflects part of the light toward the photosensitive plate.

6 When the two beams meet on the photosensitive plate, they produce a hologram or interference pattern. When the hologram is illuminated again by the reference beam, the original object image is re-created.

Science and Health

A t one time, the practice of medicine was more of an artisan's craft than a science and involved just a few tools to cure people. Around 500 years ago, due to remarkable scientific and technical advances, medicine became a technological discipline. Because of this development, life expectancies increased significantly, and remedies that before might have been considered miraculous became commonplace. Obviously the story is not over yet, and there is still much to be accomplished, but advances, such as robotic surgery, where a doctor performs surgery remotely, or the use of magnetic resonance equipment that can detect tumors in soft tissue, are very important. ●

Magnetic Resonance Imaging (MRI)

Water molecule

T hanks to a sophisticated technology that combines magnetic fields and radio waves, it is possible to render high-quality images of soft tissue in the human body without inconvenience to the patient, other than the requirement for the patient to remain still for a few minutes. Another revolutionary feature of this technique is that it does not require the use of contrast agents or the use of X-rays, as is the case for radiography or computerized tomography. ●

Inside a Scanner

To render an image of the soft tissue in the human body, the machine scans for the hydrogen atoms in these tissues. To detect the atoms, the area is initially subjected to a powerful magnetic field and later stimulated using radio-frequency waves. This process causes the atoms to release energy that is then detected by the scanner and converted into images.

Superconducting magnet

The magnet, made out of a niobium-titanium alloy, becomes a superconductor when it is cooled to -452° F (-269° C). It generates a powerful magnetic field that lines up the hydrogen protons prior to their being stimulated with the radio waves.

Cooling systems

In addition to compensating for the enormous amounts of heat generated by the electromagnetic equipment, these systems cool the main magnet to -452° F (-269° C) to turn it into a superconductor. Liquid helium is generally used as the cooling agent.

Magnetic gradient coils

generate secondary magnetic fields that, together with the superconducting magnet, enable imaging of different planes of the human body.

Radio-frequency transmitter

emits radio signals through a transmitting coil (antenna) to stimulate the hydrogen atoms that are aligned by the magnetic field. When the stimulation stops, the atoms release energy that is captured and used to form the image.

HYDROGEN IN THE BODY

Hydrogen atoms are present in almost all tissues and fluids, especially in water (which makes up 70 percent of the body) and in fat.

The hydrogen atom

is the simplest element of nature. It has just one proton (+) and one electron (-).

Electron

H

Proton

Because of its physical structure, the hydrogen atom's proton spins on its axis. This generates a magnetic field that will interact with an external magnetic field.

+

Proton

Rotation

-

A magnetic dipole is created along the axis of rotation.

Magnetic field

It also spins around a second axis, like a top, traveling within a conelike (precession) trajectory.

Precession axis

Classification

Low-energy nuclei. The spin and the precession axis rotate in the same direction.

High-energy nuclei. The spin and the precession axis rotate in opposite directions.

Planes

Magnetic resonance imaging can generate cross-sectional images at any point in the human body and in any plane.

Profile cross section

Frontal cross section

Top cross section

High Magnetism

The magnetic field generated by MRI scanners tends to be tens of thousands of times more powerful than the magnetic field of the Earth.

HUNTING FOR ATOMS

1 **Hydrogen in the body**

The axes of precession are randomly oriented in different directions.

2 **Magnetism**

A strong magnetic field helps to line up the precession axes in the same direction.

Magnetic field

3 **Stimulation**

Next, energy in the form of radio waves is applied, and low-energy protons absorb it to become high-energy protons.

Magnetic field

Radio waves

4 **Relaxation**

When transmission of radio waves stops, the low-energy protons return to their previous state. While they relax, they release the energy they have absorbed.

Magnetic field

5 **Analysis**

This released energy is interpreted by the MRI scanner to form images.

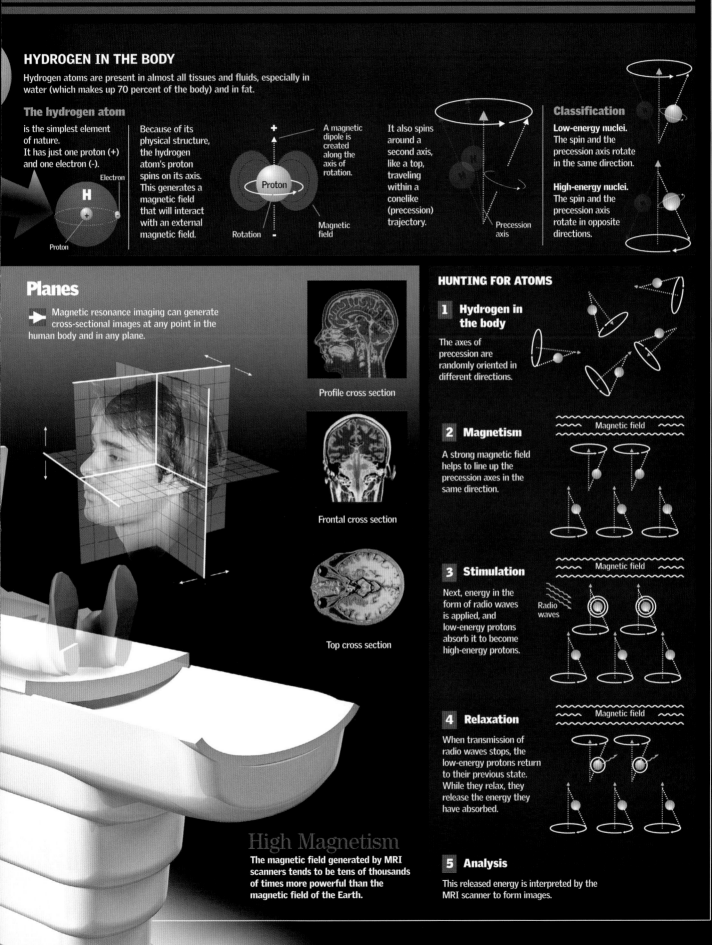

Positron Emission Tomography (PET)

Just as computed tomography and magnetic resonance imaging are well-established diagnostic methods for studying internal structures of the body, PET has in recent years become the most sophisticated technique for studying biochemical processes in patients in real time. Specialists can use it to determine how tissues in the patient's body are working and thereby obtain precise diagnoses of cancer or neurological disorders, which are difficult to determine with other methods. ●

Glucose

is the main source of energy in cells. For this reason, the study of how glucose is being used in the body tells a great deal about metabolism. Anomalies in metabolism can be related to important diseases, such as malignant tumors and Alzheimer's disease.

90%

The percentage of correct PET-derived diagnoses of cancer, including early-stage cancers

Hydrogen   **Carbon**   **Oxygen**

‹----------- In the blood -----------○

Following the Tracer

In order to study the behavior of glucose in the body, it is necessary to tag it with a tracer so that it can be detected. Glucose with a radioactive tracer is injected into the body for this purpose. It is metabolized like ordinary glucose and readily observable in a PET scan.

Glucose molecule

Fluor-18

1 The glucose molecule is treated with a radioactive isotope (a type of unstable atom). Fluor-18 is typically used, though carbon-11, oxygen-15, and nitrogen-13 can also be used.

2 The radioactively tagged glucose (in this case fluorodeoxyglucose, or FDG) is injected in the patient under study.

Luminous Collision

Once FDG is inside the body of the patient, it emits positrons as it is absorbed and metabolized. Thanks to the emission of positrons, the process can be followed in a PET scan.

Glucose molecule

3 Within the FDG molecule, fluor-18 emits positrons, which are the antimatter equivalent of electrons. In other words, positrons are electrons that have a positive instead of a negative charge.

Positron

Fluor-18

Electron

Gamma rays

Electron

Positron

Gamma rays

4 In the rest of the tissues and structures of the body, there are many free electrons that are susceptible to encountering positrons emitted by the FDG.

5 When an electron (with a negative charge) collides with a positron (with a positive charge), both particles are annihilated and all their mass changes into energy. More precisely, the mass changes into two gamma-ray photons that are emitted in opposite directions, at 180° from each other.

6 These flashes are captured and amplified in the PET scan to determine the position and concentration of FDG molecules and to track them within the patient's body. The PET scan processor then converts this information into color images.

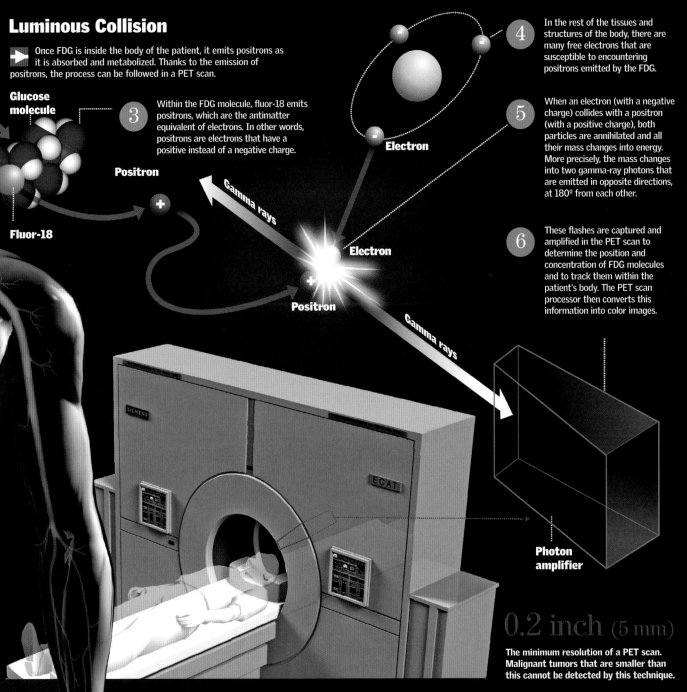

Photon amplifier

0.2 inch (5 mm)

The minimum resolution of a PET scan. Malignant tumors that are smaller than this cannot be detected by this technique.

Images

PET scans are very useful for diagnosing malignant tumors and neurological pathologies, such as Alzheimer's disease or Parkinson's disease. Whereas computed tomography can provide anatomical and structural information for internal organs, a PET scan can provide information about metabolic and biochemical activity and how medicines act.

NORMAL

This image shows the metabolic activity of a normal brain. The nerve cells consume large amounts of glucose.

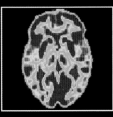

WITH ALZHEIMER'S DISEASE

This image clearly shows areas that are completely dark, indicating the low level of glucose metabolism that is characteristic of Alzheimer's disease.

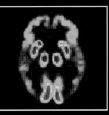

4-D Ultrasound

I s the latest word in diagnostic examinations in obstetrics. Ultrasound imaging in four dimensions incorporates time as a new variable, and it produces color images in real time that give the impression of watching a movie of a baby as it is growing inside the uterus. However, it is not a movie properly speaking but the sweep of ultrasonic waves that are reflected as echoes by the fetus. These echoes are analyzed and converted into images by powerful processors that perform mathematical calculations. The use of 4-D ultrasound has not yet been completely embraced by doctors, many of whom prefer traditional two-dimensional ultrasounds for their exams. ●

The Ultrasonic Window

The ultrasound machine uses a handheld probe that is moved over the mother's abdomen. The probe contains transducers that emit ultrasonic (high-frequency) waves that pass through the abdomen and bounce off the baby, creating echoes. These reflected waves are detected by the transducer and then converted into images.

Transducers
There are usually 128. They both emit ultrasound waves and also receive those waves that are reflected back.

5,000

The times per second that the transducer emits ultrasonic waves and detects the waves that are reflected by the fetus

Motor
turns the transducers in an 80° arc about 20 times per second.

How It Works

Although the result of the exam is a moving image of a fetus in color, the ultrasound machine does not use optical equipment but only sound waves reflected by the baby. This imaging method is generally not considered to pose a risk for the fetus or the mother.

1 Emission
The transducer emits ultrasonic waves at specific frequencies that will pass through external tissues into the uterus where the baby is. A motor varies the plane of the emitted waves many times a second to produce three-dimensional images.

2 Echo
The ultrasonic waves collide with and bounce from fetal tissues. The frequencies used are inaudible to the human ear.

3 Reception
The transducer receives the waves reflected from the tissues of the fetus. Depending on their characteristics and how they were modified, the processor extracts information from the reflected waves and converts them into moving images in real time.

20 to 20,000 hertz

The range of frequencies that humans can hear. Ultrasound imaging uses frequencies that range from 1,500,000 hertz to 60,000,000 hertz.

Fluid-filled chamber
The liquid improves the efficiency of the transmission of ultrasonic sound waves.

Development

Ultrasound imaging technology has developed in recent years from producing somewhat confusing multicolored pictures to movielike images of the fetus in the uterus.

2-D ULTRASOUND

is for obstetrics the ultrasound-imaging method par excellence. Although it is much less spectacular than more modern methods, doctors prefer it because it provides cross-sectional views of the fetus from any angle, which is helpful in examining its internal structures.

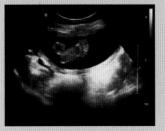

3-D ULTRASOUND

yields a static three-dimensional image of the fetus. It can be used to identify structural malformations and even facial features. The image is produced by obtaining a series of parallel cross-sectional views along the length of the fetus. These views are then processed mathematically to produce the three-dimensional image.

4-D ULTRASOUND

High-speed processors make it possible to obtain a number of 3-D ultrasound images within a fraction of a second and to perform the mathematical calculations needed to generate the images of the fetus in motion.

In Vitro Fertilization

Ever since the first successful case of in vitro fertilization in the United Kingdom almost three decades ago, this technique has become the most popular and widespread method of assisted reproductive technology. It involves removing a woman's ova, or eggs, and fertilizing them with sperm outside the woman's womb; in fact, the procedure is done in a laboratory to avoid various problems that can hinder a natural pregnancy. Once fertilized, the embryo is implanted in the uterus to continue gestation. Over time, in vitro fertilization techniques have become more efficient, and in the past few years, the number of successful pregnancies has seen a seven-fold increase. Today in vitro fertilization can be combined with other techniques to increase the chances of conception.

1,000,000

is the approximate number of babies throughout the world that have been conceived through this method since the first-known case in 1978.

UTERUS

OVARY

Egg

Pituitary gland

Generates hormones that stimulate the development of the egg

Searching for Eggs

→ The first step in achieving in vitro fertilization is to obtain good eggs in sufficient numbers to be fertilized.

1 Usually a woman produces one suitable egg each cycle (every 28 days). By using stimulating hormones, several more eggs can be obtained.

2 At this stage, the woman is monitored with ultrasound scans and blood tests to determine her hormonal levels.

3 Once they mature, the eggs are extracted through follicular aspiration. A needle connected to a suction instrument is inserted through the vagina and used to extract eggs from both ovaries.

ICSI

is the acronym for a technique known as Intracytoplasmic Sperm Injection, which has revolutionized infertility treatment in recent years. It consists of injecting the spermatozoon directly into the ovaries during in vitro fertilization.

VAGINA

A Baby Factory

▶ Once the most suitable eggs are selected, they are fertilized in a laboratory with the sperm of the future father and either inserted into the mother's uterus or frozen for use at a later time.

The semen sample obtained from the father is treated to separate the spermatozoa and to select the best ones.

The head of the spermatozoon contains DNA that, in combination with the egg's DNA, will create a new life.

Back into the Uterus

UTERUS

Days 6 to 18

Implantation

The selected embryos (usually several are selected to increase the chances of success) are transferred to the mother's uterus through a catheter inserted into the vagina.

Trophoblast
Outer cells develop the placenta.

Embryoblast
Inner cells develop the fetus.

Fertilization

takes place in a special cultivation medium in a petri dish at the same temperature as the human body.

The embryo

From this moment, the embryo is monitored and cared for by medical personnel. If it develops successfully, it will become a baby.

After 12 hours

the first cellular division takes place. The embryo now consists of two cells. The number of cells increases exponentially every 12 to 15 hours.

Day 3

When the embryo reaches between 16 and 64 cells, it is called a morula (from the Latin word *morus*, meaning "mulberry").

Day 5

When it surpasses 64 cells, the embryo becomes a blastula. A large cavity forms in the middle. At this phase, the embryo can be transferred to the woman's uterus.

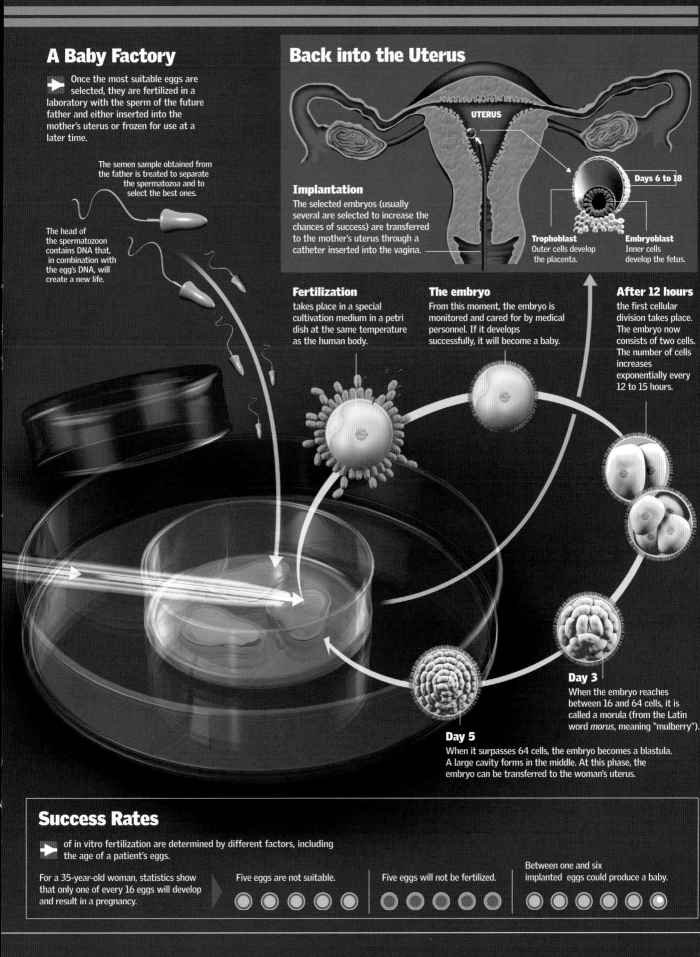

Success Rates

▶ of in vitro fertilization are determined by different factors, including the age of a patient's eggs.

For a 35-year-old woman, statistics show that only one of every 16 eggs will develop and result in a pregnancy.

Five eggs are not suitable.

Five eggs will not be fertilized.

Between one and six implanted eggs could produce a baby.

Bionic Implants

Until a few decades ago, the only option for amputees was the use of rigid and uncomfortable wood prostheses. Today at the beginning of the 21st century, the dream of being able to use artificial limbs that are connected through the nervous system—with the capability of responding to direct commands from the brain—is at the point of becoming reality. At least there are very advanced experimental prototypes along those lines, and there are already commercially available prostheses with surprising features, which in some cases are superior to human limbs.

Almost Science Fiction

The experimental bionic arm developed by the Rehabilitation Institute of Chicago is one of the most advanced models yet made. It can interpret commands from the brain so that the patient can regain the full functionality of the limb that was lost.

1 The surgeons take the nerves that were connected to the arm and redirect them to muscles of the thorax.

2 When the person fitted with the device wills an action involving the arm, such as raising the arm, the hand, or a finger, the command travels through the nerves, which produce small, precise contractions in the thorax muscles.

3 These contractions are detected by a series of sensors that transmit electrical signals to the computer in the prosthetic arm.

4 The computer then directs the motors to make the arm perform the desired motion.

Half Human, Half Machine

Among the numerous advances forthcoming in the next few years, in addition to bionic arms and legs, are: products stemming from the development of artificial veins, arteries, organs, and muscles; eyes and ears for the blind and deaf; microprocessors that enable quadriplegics to recover the use of their limbs; and even a device to eliminate chronic pain.

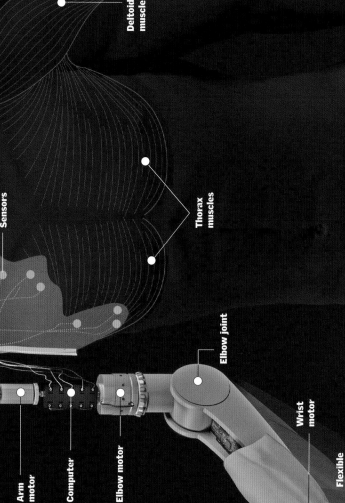

- Deltoid muscle
- Nerve
- Sensors
- Thorax muscles
- Arm elevation axis
- Arm motor
- Computer
- Elbow motor
- Elbow joint
- Wrist motor
- Flexible wrist

The Intelligent Foot

▲ In contrast to the bionic arm, the Proprio Foot (which was developed by the prosthesis company Ossur and is commercially available) does not interpret commands from the brain. Instead it reproduces the functions of the human foot by taking into account the terrain and the user's movements and gait.

Operation

A device called an accelerometer records the movement of the leg about 1,000 times each second. The computer uses the data to make the appropriate adjustments of the mechanisms in the foot.

Versatility

The Proprio Foot can turn, flex up and down, and carry out adjustments that make walking comfortable, even when going up a slope or climbing stairs—situations that tend to be difficult for amputees.

Always Alert

▲ The Proprio Foot responds, without input from the user, to such situations as being seated in a chair or going up or down stairs.

Sitting

For greater comfort, the prosthesis bends the foot so that its forward tip touches the ground.

On stairs

When the prosthesis detects two stair steps in succession, it rotates the ankle to place the foot in the proper position.

Automation

In general, it is not necessary for the user to make any adjustments because the prosthesis automatically detects and analyzes changing situations and continually makes its own adjustments.

600 million

The number of persons worldwide who have some type of disability. The figure accounts for 10 percent of the world population.

Robotic Surgery

The use of robots to perform surgeries stopped being a science-fiction fantasy and became a reality about 10 years ago, when the first surgeries of this kind were performed. During unassisted robotic surgery, the surgeon works from a computer console while a robot with special arms operates directly on the patient. This type of surgery enables the surgeon to operate remotely on patients located across the world by using a high-bandwidth connection. Robotic surgery offers numerous advantages, such as extreme precision of the incisions (hand movements are scaled and filtered to eliminate hand tremors) and the small size of incisions, which shortens recovery time for the patient and allows a given doctor to operate on a specific patient without having to be in the same physical location. ●

The Console

is where the surgeon performs the surgical procedure. The virtual-reality environment allows the doctor to observe incisions and organs magnified up to 20 times.

In spite of not operating on a patient directly, the console allows the doctor to "feel" the operation, because the robot transmits data related to flexibility, pressure, and resistance, among other information.

500,000

is the approximate number of robotic surgical procedures that have been performed since the technique was first developed in 1977.

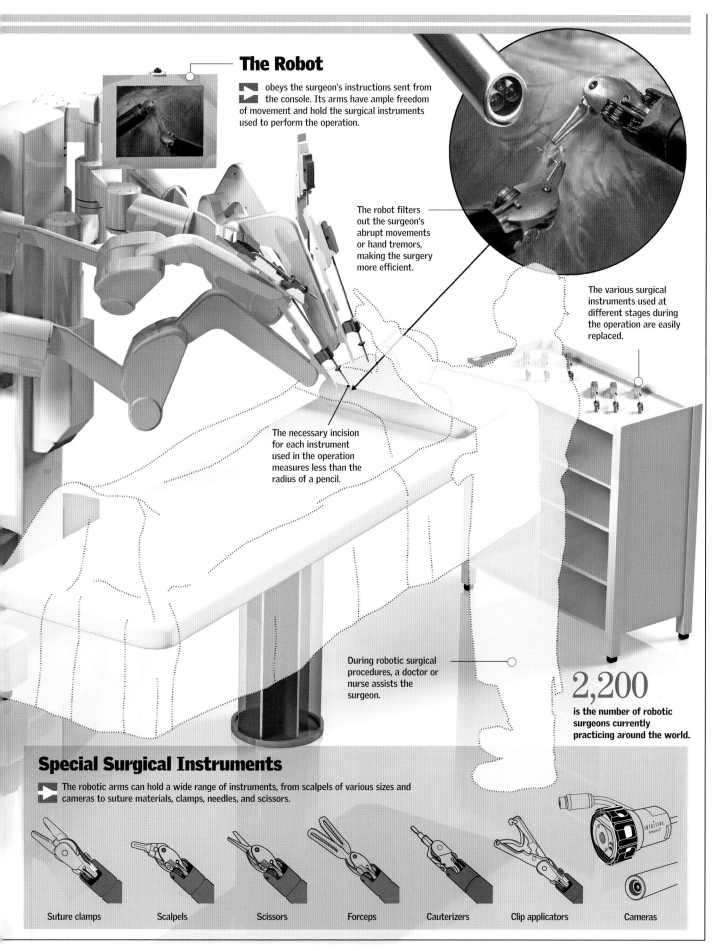

The Robot

▶▶ obeys the surgeon's instructions sent from the console. Its arms have ample freedom of movement and hold the surgical instruments used to perform the operation.

The robot filters out the surgeon's abrupt movements or hand tremors, making the surgery more efficient.

The various surgical instruments used at different stages during the operation are easily replaced.

The necessary incision for each instrument used in the operation measures less than the radius of a pencil.

During robotic surgical procedures, a doctor or nurse assists the surgeon.

2,200 is the number of robotic surgeons currently practicing around the world.

Special Surgical Instruments

▶ The robotic arms can hold a wide range of instruments, from scalpels of various sizes and cameras to suture materials, clamps, needles, and scissors.

Suture clamps | Scalpels | Scissors | Forceps | Cauterizers | Clip applicators | Cameras

Artificial Heart

The artificial heart has experienced a notable development since the first permanent artificial-heart implant in 1982, although the procedure continues to undergo experimental study because of its complexity. The most advanced artificial heart, a model called AbioCor, has been successfully implanted into a number of seriously ill heart patients, one of whom lived as long as 17 months with the device. The AbioCor heart is self-contained within the body and needs minimum maintenance. The marvel of the artificial heart is closer to becoming an everyday reality, although in the short term it is still not available for widespread use. ●

The Implant

is carried out while maintaining blood circulation by means of connections to the principal veins and arteries without using internal sutures that could hinder blood flow. The implant is a major surgical intervention.

Location

The artificial heart occupies the cavity that remains after the patient's heart has been removed during surgery. The patient's appearance is not affected.

Aorta artery

The oxygenated blood is pumped out of the heart through the aorta to the entire body.

Pulmonary artery

The heart pumps deoxygenated blood through the pulmonary artery to the lungs, where the blood is cleaned and oxygenated.

Primary valves

There are four. As with the human heart, the valves open only to allow blood to enter or leave, thereby avoiding dangerous reflux.

Material

An alloy of titanium and light plastic to which blood does not stick

Vena cava

receives blood from the body—blood that contains waste and is low in oxygen—and empties it into the right atrium of the heart.

Pulmonary vein

The cleaned blood, rich in oxygen, enters the left atrium of the heart.

How It Works

The key to the artificial heart is a compartment that has flexible walls and is filled with silicone fluid. An internal rotary motor causes the fluid to press outward, creating pressure against the flexible walls of the compartment. Valves direct this pressure, which is the secret to the proper operation of the artificial organ.

Valve motor

operates the valves that control the flow of hydraulic fluid from one side of the compartment to the other.

Rotary motor

It runs at up to 9,000 rpm to produce the centrifugal force that creates the hydraulic pressure.

PUMPING

1 The hydraulic pressure in the pump is directed against the flexible wall on one side of the pump. The wall pushes outward against an overlying chamber filled with blood and pushes the blood out of it. Meanwhile, the overlying chamber on the opposite side of the pump fills with blood.

Direction of the blood

Fluid

Pump

2 The closed valves open and the open valves close, and the hydraulic pressure is shifted to the other side of the pump. The process repeats itself over and over.

Fluid

Pump

5 years

is the anticipated survival period for patients who, in a few years, will receive the AbioCor II, a new model whose introduction is expected in 2008.

Implanted Components

Except for an external pack of batteries, all the components of the system are placed within the body of the patient and are not visible.

Outside the body

Inside the body

Transcutaneous energy transmitter

It has an external coil that sends energy through the skin to an internal reception coil; this energy is used for charging the internal batteries. This setup avoids having wires or tubes protruding through the skin and consequently reduces the risk of infection.

Heart

weighs 2 pounds (0.9 kg). It is powered by the internal batteries.

Controller

In addition to controlling the operation of the heart, it monitors the blood temperature and pressure.

Internal batteries

contain lithium. They receive energy from the external batteries and transfer it to the artificial heart.

External battery pack

also contains lithium. The pack is the only part of the system that is not implanted within the body. It is used to recharge the internal batteries.

Remote monitoring unit

It is used to monitor the operation of the artificial heart.

Cutting-Edge Technology

Today technology continues to pave the way toward the future and is beginning to change our lives and habits. Recently a number of documentaries have shown us different applications of smart technologies, technologies that are already in use in Japan, including companion robots that many families consider to be a family member. These

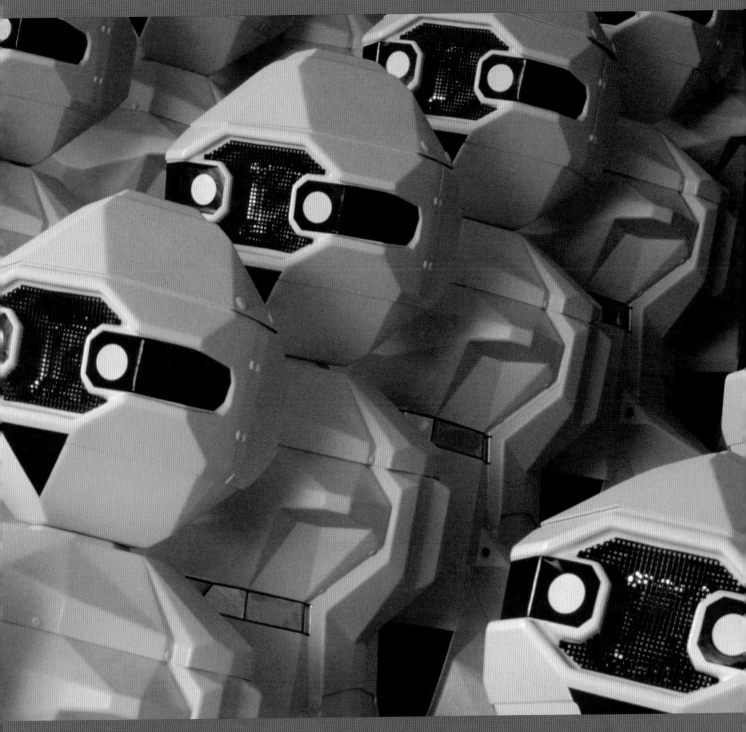

ROBOT PRODUCTION
In the future, these machines will be able to "see," which will allow them to control airports, fly planes, and drive military vehicles.

types of technological breakthroughs are only now taking off, and they still tantalize and delight us. But one thing is certain: the future is here, and we are seeing it develop in front of our own eyes. We invite you to discover the numerous applications of nanotechnology and smart clothing, new allies in the search for a higher quality of life. ●

Smart Houses

The goal of smart-house technology is to develop ways that give a house intelligence so that it can adapt on its own to the needs and wishes of the people who live in it while it also takes care of all the tasks related to home maintenance and security. Even though much of the technology that has been developed for this purpose is too expensive for most people, the continual advances made in this field suggest that in the near future almost all homes will have smart-house devices.

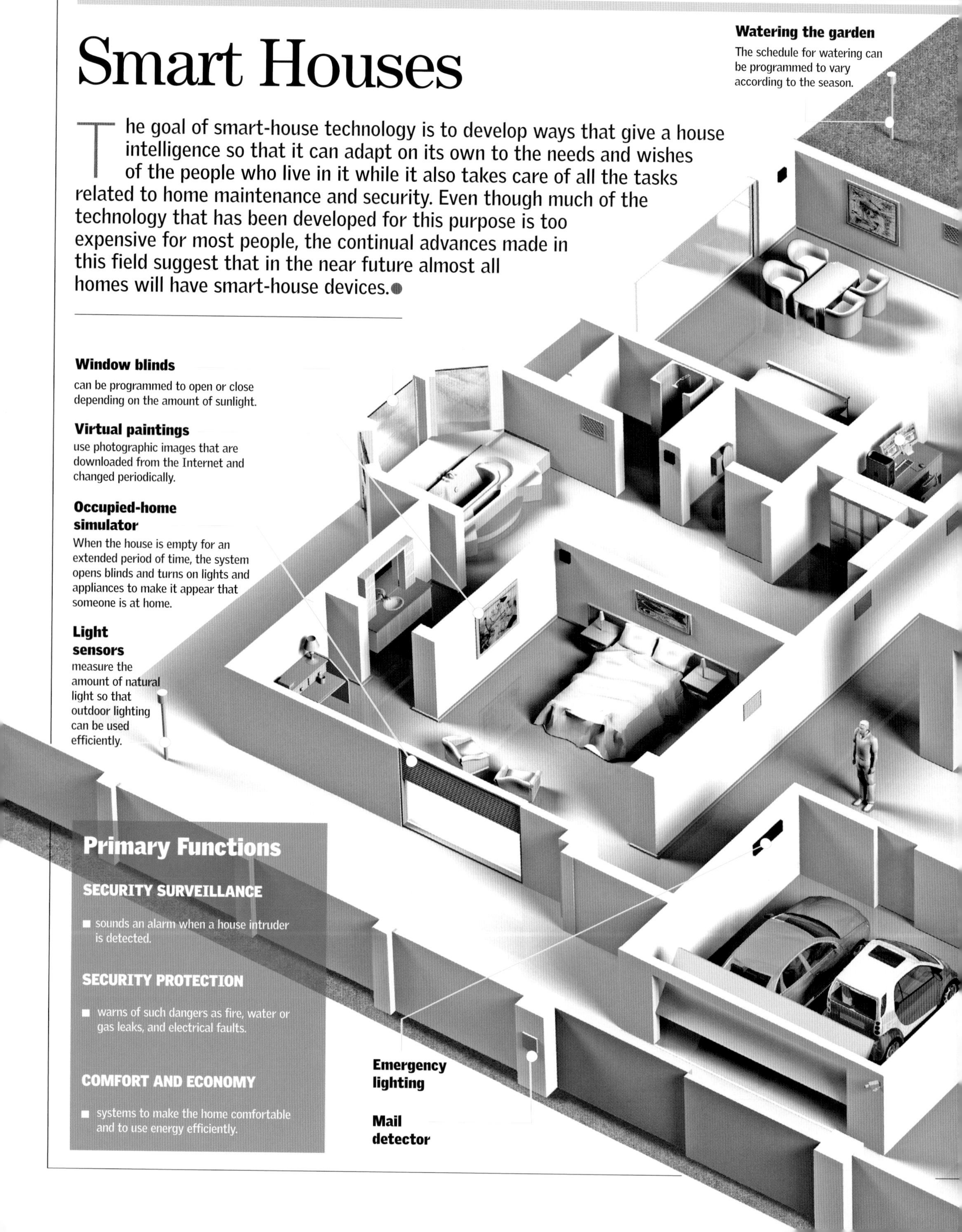

Watering the garden
The schedule for watering can be programmed to vary according to the season.

Window blinds
can be programmed to open or close depending on the amount of sunlight.

Virtual paintings
use photographic images that are downloaded from the Internet and changed periodically.

Occupied-home simulator
When the house is empty for an extended period of time, the system opens blinds and turns on lights and appliances to make it appear that someone is at home.

Light sensors
measure the amount of natural light so that outdoor lighting can be used efficiently.

Primary Functions

SECURITY SURVEILLANCE
- sounds an alarm when a house intruder is detected.

SECURITY PROTECTION
- warns of such dangers as fire, water or gas leaks, and electrical faults.

COMFORT AND ECONOMY
- systems to make the home comfortable and to use energy efficiently.

Emergency lighting

Mail detector

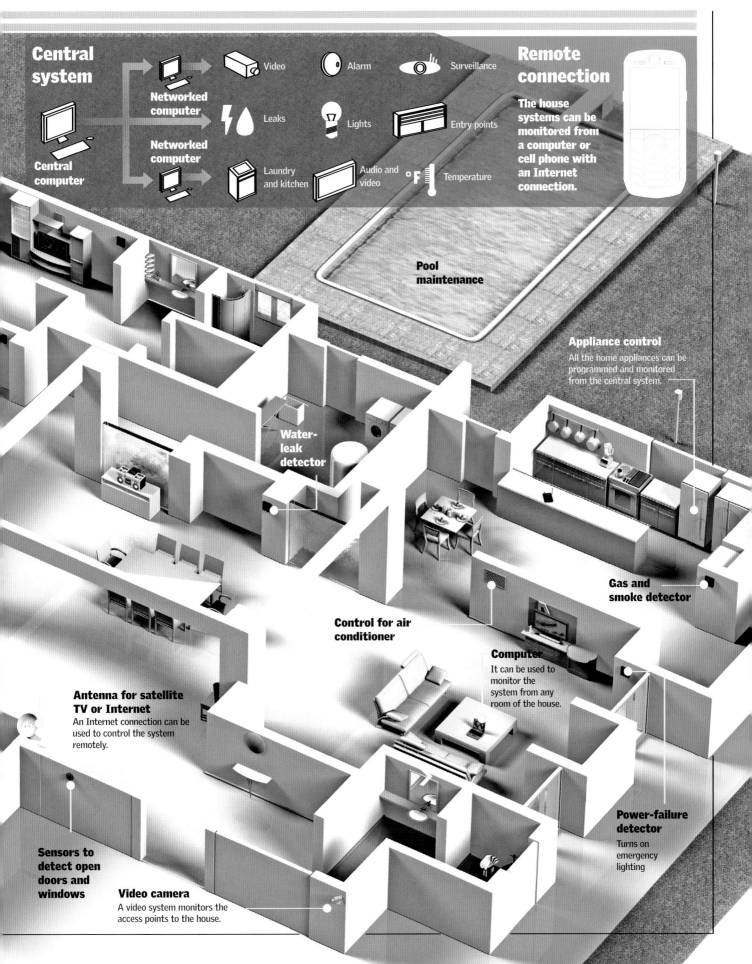

Central system

Central computer

Networked computer

Networked computer

Video

Leaks

Laundry and kitchen

Alarm

Lights

Audio and video

Surveillance

Entry points

°F Temperature

Remote connection

The house systems can be monitored from a computer or cell phone with an Internet connection.

Pool maintenance

Appliance control
All the home appliances can be programmed and monitored from the central system.

Water-leak detector

Gas and smoke detector

Control for air conditioner

Computer
It can be used to monitor the system from any room of the house.

Antenna for satellite TV or Internet
An Internet connection can be used to control the system remotely.

Power-failure detector
Turns on emergency lighting

Sensors to detect open doors and windows

Video camera
A video system monitors the access points to the house.

Nanotechnology

The term "nanotechnology" refers to the study, design, synthesis, manipulation, and application of materials, devices, and functional systems by controlling matter at the nanoscale. These new, atomically precise structures, such as carbon nanotubes or minuscule instruments to examine the inside of the human body, promise a new technological revolution still difficult to imagine. Specialists in the field expect numerous industrial, scientific, and social breakthroughs. One day, there will be materials that are more resistant than steel yet lighter, cleaner, and more efficient. Among many possible applications that could appear are computers with significantly faster components and molecular sensors capable of detecting and destroying cancer cells in the brain. ●

1 nanometer (nm)

is one-billionth of a meter, or one-millionth of a millimeter (0.04 inch). In other words, it is equivalent to dividing 1 inch into 25 million equal parts.

SOME COMPARISONS

Water molecule: **0.3 nm**

Maximum circumference of a virus

Circumference of a bacterium

Circumference of a red blood cell

Circumference of a typical human cell

Thickness of a DNA molecule: **2.5 nm**

Virus: **20-250 nm**

Bacteria: **1,000 nm**

Red blood cell: **7,000 nm**

Typical human cell: **20,000 nm**

Thickness of a hair: **80,000 nm**

Circumference of a hair

Challenges

One of the challenges researchers face is how to develop nanotubes of the longest possible length. The longest nanotube to date measures 1.5 inches (4 cm).

The Crystalline Structure

The structure formed by atoms once they align affects the properties of the material. One example is pure carbon, which, according to its structure, can become:

1 **Diamond**
Very hard, transparent mineral

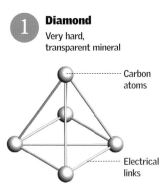

Carbon atoms

Electrical links

Infinite Applications

There exist a variety of applications for nanotechnology. The following examples are the most immediate, although most are experimental. The imagination is the only limit.

Information technology

Molecular nanoprocessors containing chips with microscopic transistors will be at the heart of computers millions of times more powerful than those that exist today.

New materials

will be dozens to hundreds of times more resistant than known materials but will also weigh much less.

Robotics

Microscopic robots (nanobots) will, for example, be able to travel inside organs and blood vessels to perform diagnostic tests and repairs.

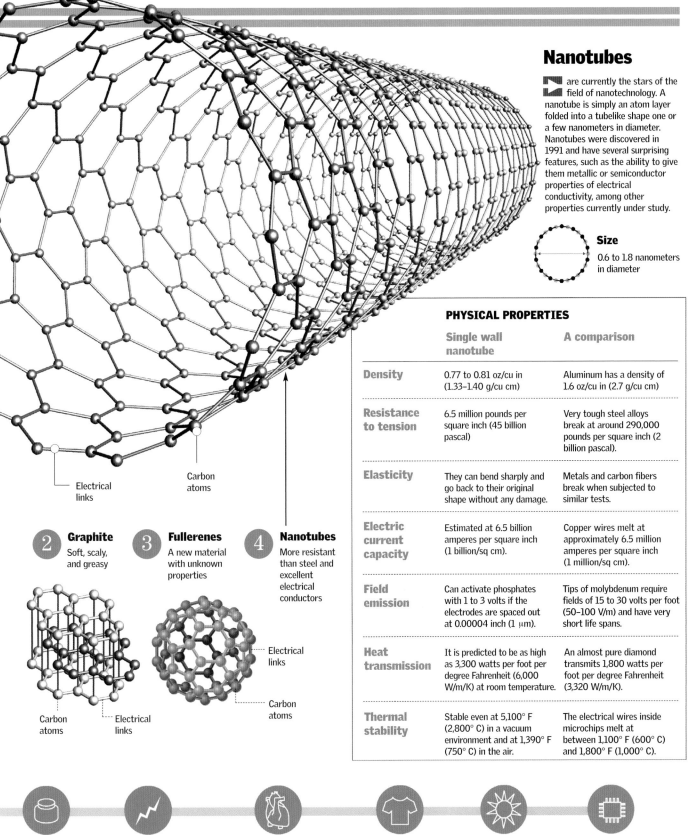

Nanotubes

are currently the stars of the field of nanotechnology. A nanotube is simply an atom layer folded into a tubelike shape one or a few nanometers in diameter. Nanotubes were discovered in 1991 and have several surprising features, such as the ability to give them metallic or semiconductor properties of electrical conductivity, among other properties currently under study.

Size
0.6 to 1.8 nanometers in diameter

Electrical links

Carbon atoms

2 **Graphite**
Soft, scaly, and greasy

3 **Fullerenes**
A new material with unknown properties

4 **Nanotubes**
More resistant than steel and excellent electrical conductors

Carbon atoms

Electrical links

Electrical links

Carbon atoms

PHYSICAL PROPERTIES

	Single wall nanotube	A comparison
Density	0.77 to 0.81 oz/cu in (1.33–1.40 g/cu cm)	Aluminum has a density of 1.6 oz/cu in (2.7 g/cu cm)
Resistance to tension	6.5 million pounds per square inch (45 billion pascal)	Very tough steel alloys break at around 290,000 pounds per square inch (2 billion pascal).
Elasticity	They can bend sharply and go back to their original shape without any damage.	Metals and carbon fibers break when subjected to similar tests.
Electric current capacity	Estimated at 6.5 billion amperes per square inch (1 billion/sq cm).	Copper wires melt at approximately 6.5 million amperes per square inch (1 million/sq cm).
Field emission	Can activate phosphates with 1 to 3 volts if the electrodes are spaced out at 0.00004 inch (1 μm).	Tips of molybdenum require fields of 15 to 30 volts per foot (50–100 V/m) and have very short life spans.
Heat transmission	It is predicted to be as high as 3,300 watts per foot per degree Fahrenheit (6,000 W/m/K) at room temperature.	An almost pure diamond transmits 1,800 watts per foot per degree Fahrenheit (3,320 W/m/K).
Thermal stability	Stable even at 5,100° F (2,800° C) in a vacuum environment and at 1,390° F (750° C) in the air.	The electrical wires inside microchips melt at between 1,100° F (600° C) and 1,800° F (1,000° C).

Cosmetics
New smart creams, particularly highly efficient sunblocks

Transmission of electrical energy
Superconducting materials that do not suffer a loss of energy during transportation at room temperature

Medicine
New medicines. Molecular and genetic repairs. Microscopic, protein-building machines, among others.

Clothing
Highly resistant, intelligent fabrics that do not get dirty or that can repel viruses and bacteria

Solar energy
Huge improvements in maximizing this clean and inexhaustible energy source

Data storage
There already exists a memory card that measures just 0.005 square inch (3 sq mm) and has a capacity of 100 gigabytes.

Smart Clothing

With the invention of smart fabrics and computerized apparel, our clothing will undergo in the coming years one of the most dramatic and surprising evolutions since humans first began wearing clothes. Some of these new breakthroughs already exist: they are showing up for the first time in the market and are becoming readily available for mass consumption. Among them are materials that integrate features that would have been hard to imagine just a few years ago–for example, clothing that not only informs the wearer of the body's response to physical activity but also modifies itself to improve performance.

Smart Fabrics

Generally a product of new developments in nanotechnology, smart fabrics show surprising features that will be widely used in the next few years.

Colorful
A special fiber made of plastic and glass can be used with electronic circuitry that modifies the way the fabric reflects light and thereby changes color.

Comfortable
Fabrics that eliminate sweat, keep the skin dry, and eliminate odors already exist. Similarly, there are materials that can provide ventilation or warmth in accordance with the outside temperature.

Resistant
Fabrics that do not get wrinkled, are resistant to stain, and keep their shape after many years of wear and washing have also been developed.

Antistatic
Fabrics that remove static electricity. They prevent the buildup of hair, pollen, dust, and other potentially harmful particles for people with allergies.

Antimicrobial
Fabrics that block the growth of viruses, fungi, bacteria, and germs

Diverse Users

Smart apparel is obviously of great benefit to athletes, but it is also important to patients with chronic illnesses, such as diabetics, who need to monitor their condition frequently.

INFORMATION IN REAL TIME

Clothes made out of fabrics with integrated minisensors and imperceptible electrical circuits can determine the wearer's heart rate, blood levels of oxygen and other gases, calories consumed, and breathing rate.

Microphone

Fiber-optic cable

Sensors

Database

Sensors

Chlorine

is an element found in the fibers of fabrics that repel germs. One of its properties is that it destroys bacterial cell walls. It is also the basis of bleach, which is frequently used in disinfectants.

Transmitter

Perfect Steps

The Adidas-1 shoe, a project three years in the making, can determine the athlete's weight, stride, and surrounding terrain to adjust the shoe's tension accordingly.

1 Inside the hollow heel, the components of the shoe generate a magnetic field.

Magnetic field

2 While running, the foot hits the heel of the shoe and modifies the magnetic field.

3 A sensor that can perform up to 1,000 readings per second detects each modification and sends that information to the microchip.

Sensor

4 A microchip determines the appropriate tension for the heel and sends the information to the motor.

5 The motor, rotating at 6,000 rpm, moves the screw, which in turn strengthens or relaxes the heel. The entire process is repeated with each step.

Heel

Sensor

Motor

Firm heel

Soft heel

5,000,000

is the number of calculations per second performed by the Adidas-1 microchip.

When a person is running, the body absorbs three to four times the person's weight each time a step is taken. Smart shoes help absorb this enormous force and protect the most vulnerable areas, and they also provide comfort and stability.

Biotechnology

The discovery during the 20th century that all the information that is needed to build a living being is found within each cell, written in a code with only four letters (the DNA molecule), led to the inevitable conclusion that the information could be artificially modified to produce new species with specific qualities or to cure hereditary diseases. Nevertheless, only in recent years have the techniques been developed to attain these objectives. The techniques have yielded products such as transgenic foods that have already become widely available in the marketplace and generated much controversy concerning safety and other issues. ●

DNA

It is an extremely long, thin molecule that holds all the information needed to form a living being. In multicellular organisms, DNA is located in the nucleus of each cell. The molecule is in the form of a chain assembled from four nucleotides, which are distinguished by their bases: adenine (A), guanine (G), cytosine (C), and thymine (T).

Pair of chromosomes

CYTOPLASM

NUCLEUS

Human Cell

Nucleus: contains genetic material

Chromosomes (23 pairs)

Cytoplasm: fluid medium with structures called organelles

Ribosomes: bodies that assemble proteins

Section of DNA

Transgenic Organisms

A transgenic organism is an organism whose genome (the set of instructions coded by its DNA) contains a gene of another species. The gene is introduced through genetic manipulation.

Plants

There are many types of transgenic plants, in particular several crops useful in agriculture. They include soy that is resistant to herbicides, corn that produces its own insecticide, and sunflowers that are tolerant to drought.

Animals

Some transgenic animals have been created to produce medical drugs on a large scale, and some have been created for laboratory experimentation. At present, there are plans to develop transgenic pigs that could produce organs for use in human transplants.

TRANSCRIPTION

1 To produce a protein, the two chains of DNA separate at the place that has the instructions to produce it.

2 The DNA code is copied by a similar type of molecule called RNA. The RNA maintains the C-G and A-T linkages (but replaces thymine with the nucleotide uracil).

3 The RNA leaves the nucleus and attaches to a ribosome, which, in accordance with the instructions encoded in the RNA, assembles amino acids to produce the specific protein.

DNA

DNA

RNA

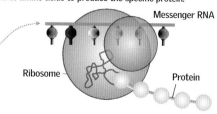

Messenger RNA

Ribosome

Protein

Cut and Paste

It is possible to "cut and paste" genes to correct genetic defects or, in the case of transgenic organisms, produce new species with selected properties.

Gene Therapies

Only the first steps have been taken in this specialized field, whose principle is to treat hereditary disorders by modifying a patient's DNA. Other illnesses, such as cancer and AIDS, might also be treatable with this type of therapy.

1 Gene therapy typically makes use of retroviruses to modify a person's DNA. Retroviruses can infect a human cell and use their RNA to modify the cell's DNA to convert the cells into a "virus factory." This capability is used to modify a cell's DNA in a desired way.

2 The retrovirus RNA is modified to reduce or eliminate its ability to cause disease. At the same time, an RNA fragment is added that is intended for insertion into the human cell.

Human Genome

A thorough understanding of the human genome and of the germs that can infect and modify it will make it possible to produce medications that are highly efficient and even tailored to the individual.

3 The retrovirus introduces its modified genetic material into the human cell.

The cell functions according to its new instructions.

NUCLEUS

Chromosome

Ribosome

CYTOPLASM

CELL

VIRUS

3 billion

The approximate number of DNA base pairs that make up the human genome

Structure

Discovered in 1953, the structure is a double helix whose strands are bridged by bases in an established pattern.

Cytosine ⬤━⬤ Guanine

Adenine ⬤━⬤ Thymine

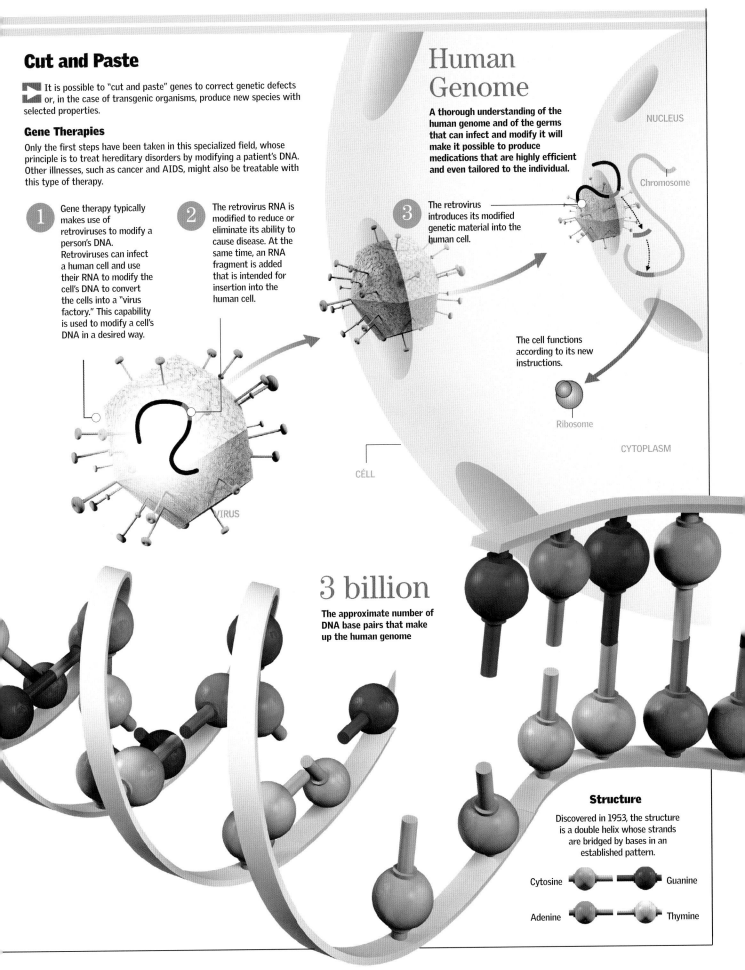

Artificial Intelligence

Although the concept of artificial intelligence (AI) had long been present in science fiction, its theoretical basis was not established until the early 1950s. At first, investigators in the discipline tackled the problem with great optimism, but over the years the challenge of creating a machine that could "feel" and behave like a human being with a capacity for abstraction—and on occasion act in an illogical manner—revealed its considerable complexity. Today there are amazing robots that still lack these human qualities. ●

Man's Best Friend

AIBO is one of the most complex robot pets ever created. According to Sony Corp, which introduced the robot in 1999, AIBO interacts with its owner, conveys emotions by wagging its tail when it is happy, or seeks attention when it is being ignored. For the present, manufacture has ceased, and customers anticipate a more advanced product.

Touch

The robot dog is sensitive to touch; it can also recognize its owner.

Multitalented

It can move around without bumping into obstacles, and it can imitate typical dog motions, such as lying down and sniffing the ground with its nose. It has its favorite toys and favorite spots around the house.

Dimensions

12.5 inches (31.7 cm)
10.9 inches (27.8 cm)

LEDS

AIBO conveys emotions through its body movements. It also uses LED patterns to communicate with its owner.

Emotions

Happy	Angry	Sad

Expressions

Recognized its owner	Detected an obstacle	Has been petted

Favorites

Petted by its owner	Favorite spot	Favorite things

AI Development

The search for artificial intelligence began in the 1950s. Since then, a number of milestones have been reached. Following are some major milestones.

1950

The Turing test is published. The purpose of the test is to determine whether a machine can be considered intelligent. The challenge consists of having a person converse with a machine and a human being at the same time. If the person cannot decide which interlocutor is the human being, the machine has passed the test. For the time being, no machine has succeeded in doing so.

1956

The researcher John McCarthy coins the term "artificial intelligence" at a celebrated Dartmouth Conference.

1962

Unimation, the first company dedicated to producing robots, is formed. Four years later a computer program called ELIZA becomes available. The program uses a dialogue system that simulates a psychotherapist's speech. According to many users/patients, this system can elicit strong emotions from them.

1973

Freddy, a robot capable of identifying and assembling objects, comes into being at the University of Edinburgh, Scotland.

1994

The twin cars VaMP and VITA-2, developed by the University of Munich and Mercedes Benz, drive under automatic control, carrying live passengers about 620 miles (1,000 km) around Paris, in traffic, at speeds up to 80 miles per hour (130 km/h).

1996

The chess program Deep Blue wins a game of chess against world chess champion Garry Kasparov.

The Day a Machine Beat the Best Human

February 10, 1996, is a red-letter day in the history of artificial intelligence. On that day, an IBM computer called Deep Blue won a game of chess in a match against the world chess champion, Garry Kasparov, becoming thereby the first computer to triumph over a reigning world champion. The game was part of a match in which the Russian player prevailed four to two.

In 1997, a rematch was held between Kasparov and Deep Blue, which won by a score of 3.5 to 2.5.

200 million

The possible number of positions evaluated each second by the improved version of Deep Blue that defeated world-chess champion Garry Kasparov

The robot can run at a speed of 3.7 miles (6 km) per hour and walk at 1.7 miles (2.7 km) an hour.

It has a 52-volt lithium-ion battery mounted in its backpack.

ASIMO

HONDA

Humanoids

Their humanlike appearance could spark our imagination and reinforce the impression that the humanoid is a living machine. At present, commercially sold humanoids serve only as a source of entertainment.

PAPERO

Produced by NEC, PaPeRo is a domestic robot that can recognize the faces of its family members, distinguish colors, read text, dance, and change a TV channel when its owner gives a verbal command. It can tell stories to children, and, by means of its camera eyes, it can send parents images of their children while the parents are at the office.

15.2 inches (38.5 cm)

The robot can lift up to 1 pound (0.5 kg) in each hand.

ASIMO

Honda's bipedal robot ASIMO (Advanced Step in Innovative Mobility) was introduced at the Robodex 2000 exhibition in Yokohama. It can walk, dance, shake hands, carry a tray of drinks like a waiter, and answer simple questions. The current model is about 4 feet 3 inches (1.3 m) tall and weighs 119 pounds (54 kg).

1998

Furby, a small pet that resembles a gremlin, is introduced. It can learn to talk as it grows up. It becomes a retail sensation.

1999

Cynthia Breazeal designs Kismet, one of the first robots to respond to people in a natural manner.

2003

QRIO
A robot made by Sony, QRIO was the first bipedal robot capable of running.
It can run at a speed of 45 ft (14 m) per minute.

Virtual Reality

I s a technology in full development whose object is to deceive the senses to create a variety of sensations. It has many applications, which have not yet been completely explored. The focus has been on forms of entertainment in which the player acts within the created setting and on simulators for training soldiers, pilots, surgeons, and others in extreme situations without placing the trainees at risk. Other promising areas for virtual reality—which combines the capabilities of the most powerful computers with ingenious mechanical devices—are in medicine (especially in the areas of treating phobias and traumas), marketing, and publicity. ●

Images

are created by powerful processors that use various 3-D programming languages. VRML is one of the most widely used, although it is giving way to X3-D, which is more complex.

HOW THEY ARE GENERATED

1 Modeling
The form of the object is generated and given a skeleton framework that, when animated, can be used to modify the shape and position of the object.

2 Composition
Textures, colors, and lighting are applied, all of which help provoke sensations of greater realism.

3 Programming
The user of the simulation needs to be able to interact with the object by means of the specific characteristics assigned to it.

Requirement

For many years, airline pilots have been required to practice periodically in flight simulators, one of the most widespread applications of virtual reality.

HELMET
generates 3-D images using complex calculations while it changes perspectives according to the head movements of the person experiencing the simulation.

DATA GLOVE
Uses electromagnetic and inertial sensors to register hand and arm movements, which are converted into electrical signals and incorporated into the simulation.

Deceiving the Senses

SIGHT
There are several means by which high-quality virtual reality misleads the sense of sight. These means include the use of special helmets and glasses and of screens that extend beyond the visual field, such as those employed in IMAX theaters.

SOUND
The challenge is to produce three-dimensional sound that simulates environmental sound. It is necessary to calculate the position of an individual with respect to the virtual sound source and objects. Good-quality simulations exist, but work remains to be done.

SMELL
Virtual-reality simulations have been developed that use strong basic odors, but they are expensive. Producing the sensation of softer and more complex aromas remains a long-term goal.

TOUCH
Some systems use gloves that can give the wearer the perception that virtual objects are present to the touch. However, a good simulation should at the same time include sensations of temperature, shape, firmness, and force—something that remains a distant goal.

TASTE
There have not been advances with this sense. It is believed that to generate taste sensations, it will be necessary to stimulate the brain directly with invasive methods akin to the neuronal sockets envisioned in the movie *Matrix*.

Passage to a Parallel World

Although the perfect virtual-reality setting remains to be created, there are those who already experience new sensations by simply putting on a helmet, a pair of gloves, and special boots.

EARPHONES

are designed to simulate 3-D sound by such techniques as delaying sound output from different channels by a fraction of a second to create the perception that sound sources are situated at distinct locations.

Textures

Researchers recognize that textures are some of the most difficult sensations to simulate. An experimental system that simulates the texture of various grades of sandpaper has been developed in the United States.

Controllers

The most advanced are wireless and detached—that is, unlike a conventional joystick, the controls are not mounted in any kind of structure. They transmit signals to the unit's processor with infrared radiation, and they can register placement, movement, speed, and acceleration through an inertial system.

$739,000,000

was the amount collected worldwide for the movie *Matrix Reloaded* (the final movie of the *Matrix* trilogy), making it one of the top 25 box-office hits of all time.

BOOTS

function like data gloves by providing information for the simulation. The boots indicate whether the user is running, walking, or resting.

Evolution

In almost half a century of evolution, virtual reality has progressed from an ingenious cinematic machine to a very promising complex technology.

1968

Morton Heilig, a cinematographer, constructs the Sensorama. The viewer sits in a chair that can vibrate. The viewer is surrounded by three screens on which a film, such as a bicycle trip through New York City, is projected. It produces smells, currents of air, and other effects. It was the first virtual-reality simulator.

1968

Ivan Sutherland, a pioneering computer scientist, proposes the use of a video display that can be placed on a viewer's head and respond to the head's orientation to make simulations more real. The result is the head-mounted display (HMD), whose early models use mirrors in a dual-projection system.

The 1980s

1977: The first data glove is patented.

Major development takes place in fighter-aircraft simulators to train pilots using HMD.

1989: The U.S. Department of Defense creates SimNet, a simulation system to train troops.

The 1990s

Many experimental approaches to touch and smell simulators are developed while simulations for vision and sound are perfected.

Perfect Simulation

The *Matrix* trilogy, whose first movie premiered in 1999, presents an idealized virtual reality. It takes place in a world dominated by machines in which human beings live in a fictitious universe. Their brains are connected to a virtual-reality machine that creates such perfect simulations that they cannot even suspect that they inhabit an illusory world.

Soldiers of the Future

For centuries, nations have devised highly diverse means of arming and defending their soldiers. With current developments, the tendency has almost been to think of a soldier as a robotic unit, one that is in constant communication with its fellow soldiers and equipped for combat in any type of terrain, environment, or condition, using weapons that are ever more precise and lethal. Despite these advances, however, the main challenge continues to be that of dealing with the vulnerability of the soldier. Within the most modern uniforms and advanced fighting systems, there is still a human being. In this regard, developments in nanotechnology that could lead to the creation of intelligent uniforms would be truly revolutionary. ●

Land Warrior

is a term used to refer to the most modern and technological approach to equipping a ground soldier. It saw limited use in the Iraq War, but the weight of the equipment and its relatively short battery life led to the suspension of the program. Newer technologies were under study to improve it.

Infrared sensors
can detect persons in absolute darkness by the heat they emit.

Camera sight
The image it produces can be viewed directly in the helmet.

Multiple antennas
receive and emit signals for radio, GPS, video, and other types of information. The soldier remains in constant contact with other soldiers in the unit, which helps prevent feelings of isolation.

Control unit
The soldier uses it to control all the systems.

Monocular screen
can show the soldier position maps and the placement of troops, among other things. It can also show images from unmanned vehicles.

Modular ceramic vest
Divided into plates, it protects the soldier from projectiles the size of an M16 round.

Energy for the system
The system is equipped with lithium batteries and can operate for 24 hours.

Mask
protects against biological and chemical weapons.

Waterproof material
maintains normal body temperature, even in extreme conditions.

Purification system for food and water
provides a constant supply of potable water and of canned or dried rations, with a menu of 24 items.

$2 billion

The cost of developing the Land Warrior project over 10 years. Arming each soldier costs less than $30,000.

Boots
Lighter and reduce rubbing

Unmanned Vehicles

have been designed to provide support, firepower, and reconnaissance without the presence of a human.

COUGAR
Unmanned ground attack vehicle. It provides a high level of firepower without risking the lives of human occupants.

60 hours

is the maximum autonomous flight time of a few types of UAVs (unmanned aerial vehicles). UAVs can perform very abrupt maneuvers that a human crew would not be able to tolerate.

Future Force Warrior

is a planning program for soldiers of the next decade. Various technological systems for defense, vision, and detection will be integrated in the helmet, and the development of nanotechnology could lead to "intelligent" uniforms.

HELMET
integrates infrared vision systems, heat sensors, sensors for chemical and biological weapons, and night-vision cameras. It has a head-up display that the soldier can use to monitor the surrounding area.

Weaponry
Precision bullets that are aimed at a target by detecting body heat

Intimidation

In addition to having lethal systems and weapons, technological soldiers can with their appearance alone produce a psychological impact on the enemy.

Uniform
Lightweight and waterproof, the uniform maintains body temperature and can change color depending on the terrain.

Sensors for detecting toxins. A microchip uses the information to release specific antidotes to protect the soldier.

Biological detectors to monitor such readings as the soldier's blood pressure and pulse

Automatic treatment of wounds by means of intelligent cloth

Masking of body temperature to evade enemy infrared sensors

Gecko technology to help the soldier climb walls

Boot
could be used to store energy from movements by means of kinetic cells.

MULE
A terrestrial vehicle designed for a variety of uses that include transportation, mine detection, and assistance providing air support.

In the Long Term

Although most of these systems are currently under development, it is unlikely that they will constitute part of regular-issue military equipment before the first 25 years of the 21st century.

- **Edible vaccines**
- **Food with biomarkers that help in identifying troops remotely**
- **High-nutrition food bars**
- **Uniforms with protein coating** provide shielding from enemy sensors.
- **Biometric sensors** constantly monitor physiological indicators.

- **Clothing to stop bleeding** applies precise pressure on a wounded part of the body.
- **Improved metabolism** can improve the oxygen supply to specific tissues and provide supplementary energy to specific cells.
- **Thermophysiology** Technology for precisely controlling body temperature

UAV
Small reconnaissance and surveillance aircraft. Some versions can carry armament to attack specific targets.

Space Exploration

B y the end of the 20th century, all the planets of the solar system had been visited by space probes, including Uranus and Neptune, the most distant planets. In some cases, the visit was only a flyby mission, which nevertheless provided data impossible to obtain from the Earth. Other missions have involved placing space probes in orbit around a planet. Yet other missions have landed probes on Venus, Mars, and Titan (one of Saturn's moons). In 1969, humans succeeded in walking on the Moon, and there are now plans to send humans to the planet Mars. ●

Unmanned Spacecraft

All planetary missions have been accomplished with unmanned spacecraft. When possible their voyages have taken advantage of the gravitational field of one or more planets in order to minimize fuel requirements.

Space Shuttle

The manned spacecraft that has been used the most since its first launching in 1981. The shuttle, however, cannot go beyond a 430-mile (700-km) Earth orbit.

Space Shuttle

International Space Station

Earth

Many artificial satellites and manned missions have orbited and continue to orbit the Earth. The orbiting International Space Station always has a crew onboard.

Moon

The Apollo missions (1969-72) took a total of 12 astronauts to the surface of the Moon. They are the only missions that have taken humans beyond the Earth's orbit. The United States and China are preparing new manned missions to the Moon.

Mercury

Visited in 1974-75 by Mariner 10 on three flybys, with a closest approach of 203 miles (327 km). The probe mapped 45 percent of the planet and made various types of measurements. In 2011, the probe Messenger will enter orbit around Mercury after making flybys in 2008 and 2009.

Venus

The most visited celestial body after the Moon, Venus has been studied by orbiting spacecraft and by landers, many in the 1970s and 1980s. During the Vega and Venera missions and the Mariner and Magellan missions, the surface of the planet was mapped and even excavated, and the atmosphere was analyzed. At present, the spacecraft Venus Express is studying the planet from orbit.

Distance from the Sun	Mercury	Venus	Earth	Mars
36,000,000 miles (57,000,000 km)	67,000,000 miles (108,000,000 km)	93,000,000 miles (150,000,000 km)	141,600,000 miles (227,900,000 km)	

Jupiter

The giant of the solar system was visited for the first time by Pioneer 10 in 1973. Another seven spacecraft (Pioneer 11, Voyagers 1 and 2, Ulysses, Cassini, Galileo, and New Horizons) have made flybys of the planet since then. Galileo studied Jupiter and its moons for eight years from 1995 to 2003, and it transmitted images and data of incalculable scientific value.

Uranus

In 1986, Uranus was visited by Voyager 2, which took photographs and readings of the planet. It is the only mission that has reached Uranus.

Neptune

The distant blue giant has been visited only once, in 1989, by Voyager 2.

7 years

The time it took for the Cassini probe to travel from the Earth as far as Jupiter. Galileo reached Jupiter in six years.

Saturn

Only four missions have visited Saturn. The first three—Pioneer 11 (1979), Voyager 1 (1980), and Voyager 2 (1981)—flew by at distances of 21,000 to 220,000 miles (34,000 to 350,000 km) from the planet. Cassini, in contrast, was placed in orbit around Saturn in 2004, and it has obtained amazing images of the planet and its rings. Part of the Cassini mission was to launch the Huygens probe, which successfully landed on the surface of Saturn's mysterious moon Titan.

Beyond the Solar System

Having left behind the orbit of Neptune, the space probes Pioneer 10 and 11 and Voyager 1 and 2 are bound for the edge of the solar system.

Eros

In 2000, the probe NEAR entered orbit around the asteroid 433 Eros. In 1986, six spacecraft, among them Giotto, reached Halley's Comet.

Pioneer 10 and 11

They were launched in 1972 and 1973 and visited Jupiter and Saturn. Contact with the probes was lost in 1997 and 1995, respectively. They carry a plaque with information about the Earth and human beings in anticipation that they may eventually be found by an extraterrestrial civilization. Pioneer 10 is headed toward the star Aldebaran, which it will reach in 1,700,000 years.

Voyager 1 and 2

Launched in 1977, they carry a gold-plated disk with music, greetings in various languages, sounds and photographs from the Earth, and scientific explanations. The probes passed Jupiter, Saturn, Uranus, and Neptune and remain in contact with the Earth. Some data indicate that in 2003 Voyager 1 might have crossed the heliopause, which is at the outer reaches of the solar system.

Mars

In 1965, Mariner 4 took the first 22 close-up images of Mars. Since then the planet has been visited by many orbiters and by probes that have landed on its surface. Among the most noteworthy are the missions of Viking (1976), Mars Pathfinder (1997), Mars Global Surveyor (1997), and the Mars Exploration Rovers (2004).

Mars Exploration Rover (2004)

Jupiter	Saturn	Uranus	Neptune
483,000,000 miles (778,000,000 km)	887,000,000 miles (1,427,000,000 km)	1,780,000,000 miles (2,870,000,000 km)	2,800,000,000 miles (4,500,000,000 km)

Extrasolar Planets

or centuries, there has been speculation about the possible existence of planets orbiting other stars in the universe in the same way that the planets of the solar system, including the Earth, revolve around the Sun. Nevertheless, it has been only a little more than a decade since it has been possible to detect such bodies—albeit indirectly—thanks to new telescopes and measuring devices with increased sensitivity. The confirmation of the existence of these extrasolar planets suddenly increases the possibility that life might exist in other corners of the cosmos. ●

Distant Worlds

▶ By late 2007, astronomers had detected more than 225 possible planets in about 200 extrasolar planetary systems. These figures indicate that many of these extrasolar planets form part of a system in which, like the solar system, more than one planet is in orbit around a star.

GASEOUS PLANETS

Almost all the extrasolar planets detected to date are gaseous giants like those of the solar system—Jupiter, Saturn, Uranus, and Neptune.

The First Photograph?

In 2004, photographs were taken that might be the first images of stars with extrasolar planets, namely 2M1207b and GQ Lup b (shown in photo). However, it is still under discussion whether these small bodies are true planets or brown dwarfs.

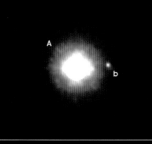

A
b

1.2 days

The time it takes the planet OGLE-TR-56 to orbit its star; it is the shortest orbital period known for a planet.

Notable Extrasolar Planets

▶ Among the extrasolar planets that have been detected, there are surprising differences in their characteristics.

The First	The Hottest	The Most Massive	The Smallest	The Closest	The Most Distant
Pegasi 51 b	HD 149026 b	Undetermined	Gliese 581 c	Epsilon Eridani b	OGLE- 2003 -BLG-235
Discovered in 1995, it was the first extrasolar planet found orbiting a normal star. It is a gaseous planet that has about one-half the mass of Jupiter and lies 47.9 light-years from the Earth.	This gaseous planet is similar to Saturn in terms of mass but smaller in size. It orbits its star at 25th the distance of the Earth from the Sun, and its surface temperature may be more than 2,700° F (1,500° C).	There are several large planetary bodies that are as much as 11 times as massive as Jupiter. Planet-sized objects with a mass above this value are considered to be almost starlike bodies; they are called brown dwarfs and their classification is in question.	Located about 20 light-years from the solar system, it is one of the extrasolar planets thought most likely to resemble the Earth. Its diameter is only 50 percent larger than that of the Earth.	This gaseous Jupiter-sized giant orbits the star Epsilon Eridani, which has characteristics similar to the Sun, although it is somewhat smaller and not as bright. It is only 10.5 light-years from the solar system.	This planet was discovered in 2004 by means of a phenomenon called gravitational microlensing. It is a gaseous giant that revolves around a star at a distance four times greater than that between the Earth and the Sun, and it is about 19,000 light-years away.

STAR

Planetary systems have been found around almost every type of star, including binary and tertiary stars and stars of various sizes and temperatures, a fact that considerably increases the possibility that some planetary systems might be inhabited.

ROCKY PLANETS

With just a few exceptions, the instruments currently used are not able to detect rocky planets like the Earth or Mars. These are the types of planets sought by astronomers, since they are the most likely to be home to life.

12.7 billion years

The age of planet PSR B1620-26b, the oldest of all the known extrasolar planets; this planet orbits a system of binary pulsars. The much-younger Earth is "only" about five billion years old.

A World Similar to the Earth

Of the many extrasolar planets reported by astronomers, Gliese 581 c is the world most like the planet Earth. It orbits a red dwarf star, and it is believed that it might have the basic conditions for the development of life.

EARTH

- **Size:** 7,930 miles (12,756 km) in diameter
- **Mass:** 13.17 x 1024 pounds (5.976 x 1024 kg)
- **Distance from its star:** 93 million miles (150 million km), or 1 AU
- **Temperature:** between -112° and 122° F (-80° and 50° C)
- **Orbital period:** 365 days
- **Water:** in gaseous, liquid, and solid states

GLIESE 581 c

- **Size:** 1.5 times the diameter of the Earth
- **Mass:** 4.83 times the Earth's mass
- **Distance from its star:** One 14th the distance of the Earth from the Sun (0.07 AU)
- **Temperature:** unknown, but believed to be between 27° and 104° F (-3° and 40° C)
- **Orbital period:** 13 days
- **Water:** It would have conditions suitable for the existence of liquid water.

Indirect Detection

The extrasolar planets are dark bodies very distant from the solar system, and they always lie in the glare of the star that they orbit. Therefore, they can generally only be detected by indirect methods, because "seeing" the planet is at present almost impossible.

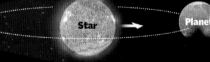

SPECTRUM SHOWING REDSHIFT

1 The gravitational force of the planet causes a slight movement of the star toward the planet. The spectrum of the light from the star will show a redshift, which indicates that star is moving away from the Earth.

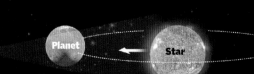

SPECTRUM SHOWING BLUESHIFT

2 When the planet is situated at the opposite side of its orbit, the spectrum of the star will show a blueshift, which indicates that the star is moving toward the Earth.

This process repeats itself over and over, revealing the existence of a planet. For the movement of a planet's star to be noticeable, the planet must exert an appreciable gravitational force, which for the present means that it is only possible to detect planets that have at least four times the Earth's mass.

Tunneling Microscope

M any applications of nanotechnology continue to be explored and developed, but it was the development of the scanning tunnel microscope (STM) that made it possible to see atoms and molecules for the first time. However, this marvelous machine, whose operation is based on the quantum-mechanical concept known as the tunneling effect, is also a powerful tool. Researchers are beginning to use this new tool in the surprising new technology of manipulating individual atoms and molecules to construct novel materials and structures at a nanometer scale. ●

The Art of Seeing the Small

▶ With the invention of the optical microscope by the early 17th century, it was possible for the first time to overcome the limitations of vision to peer into the world at ever-smaller scales. This invention was followed by the electron microscope, invented around the middle of the 20th century. With the introduction of the scanning tunneling microscope in the 1980s, it was finally possible to image individual atoms.

HUMAN EYE
▦ **Resolution: one tenth of a millimeter**

OPTICAL MICROSCOPE

Uses visible light focused by lenses. The microscope's resolution is limited by the size of the wavelengths of light.

| ⊕ **Magnification** up to 2,000 times | ▦ **Resolution:** 200 nanometers | ◉ **Images:** transparent, two dimensional |

TRANSMISSION ELECTRON MICROSCOPE

It illuminates the sample with focused beams of electrons—that is, it uses shorter wavelengths than those of visible light and thereby overcomes light's limitation.

| ⊕ **Magnification** up to 1,000,000 times | ▦ **Resolution:** 0.5 nanometers | ◉ **Images:** transparent, two dimensional |

SCANNING ELECTRON MICROSCOPE

scans the sample with a beam of electrons and reads the surface.

| ⊕ **Magnification** of up to 1,000,000 times | ▦ **Resolution:** 10 nanometers | ◉ **Images:** opaque, three dimensional |

SCANNING TUNNELING MICROSCOPE

Based on quantum principles, it makes atomic-scale imaging possible.

| ⊕ **Magnification** of up to 1,000,000,000 times | ▦ **Resolution:** 0.001 nanometer (vertical) and 0.1 nanometer (horizontal) | ◉ **Images:** three-dimensional graphical images of atomic structures |

THE TUNNELING CURRENT

is a current of electrons that pass between the sample and probe by means of the tunneling effect. The current is generated by applying a voltage between the sample and the probe. The intensity of the current varies according to the distance between the tip of the probe and the sample—in other words, according to the relief of the sample.

Nobel Prize

The physicists Gerd Binnig (German) and Heinrich Rohrer (Swiss) in 1981 established the theoretical groundwork for the development of the STM. For this work they were awarded the Nobel Prize for Physics in 1986.

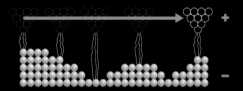

THE STM PROBE

The tip of the probe is an electrical conductor that is free of oxides and comes to as sharp a point as possible—ideally a single atom.

THE SAMPLE

for an STM must be either metallic or a semiconductor, and it must be very smooth. Its surface roughness should be less than one thousandth of a millimeter.

The STM in Action

To see atoms the STM reads the surface of an object with an extremely fine point, comparable to the way a person can use the tip of a finger to read Braille by detecting patterns of raised dots.

The process for reading the surface at an atomic scale requires producing a tunneling current between the STM probe and the sample. For this reason, the entire microscope functions like an electrical circuit.

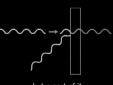

The Tunneling Effect

is quantum-mechanical in nature. There is nothing analogous on the scale of humans and everyday objects.

IN CLASSICAL PHYSICS

a particle cannot pass through an energy barrier (a potential barrier) if the energy of the barrier is greater than that of the particle.

IN QUANTUM MECHANICS

a particle does not have a concrete location. Instead, the particle has wavelike properties and its position is defined in terms of a probability cloud, which extends beyond the barrier. In this way, the particle can cross the barrier by, in effect, tunneling through it.

The wave is reflected by the wall

but a part of it can pass through.

Thanks to the tunneling effect, electrons pass from the STM probe to the sample despite the barrier presented by the vacuum between them. The strength of this tunneling current is measured to determine the placement of the atoms on the sample being studied.

The Result

is a graphic that shows the peaks and valleys of the sample's atomic and electronic structure.

The processor converts the variations in tunneling-current intensity registered by the probe into graphics that represent the atomic structure at the surface of the sample.

Manipulation of Atoms

One of the most astonishing applications of STM is the manipulation of individual atoms and molecules as building blocks in microscopic constructions. This experimental technology might lead to the creation of new materials with unsuspected properties.

1 The probe is first used in its scanning mode to identify the atom to be moved.

2 The tip approaches the atom until it almost touches. The attractive forces generated by the tip of the probe can then pull the atom along the surface of the sample.

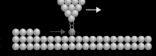

3 The strength of the probe's electrical field is reduced to release the atom into the desired position.

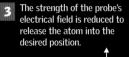

Hadron Collider

he Large Hadron Collider (LHC) is a very large scientific instrument at the European Organization for Nuclear Research (CERN). It is installed in an underground tunnel that is in the form of a ring about 5.3 miles (8.5 km) in diameter and underlies the border between France and Switzerland. The function of the instrument is to make particles collide with great energy to break them apart and obtain data concerning the basic forces of the universe. This information can lead to the discovery of new elementary particles as well as confirm the presence of elementary particles whose existence has only been determined theoretically. ●

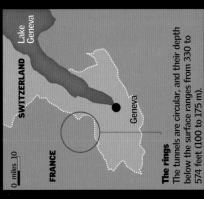

FRANCE

SWITZERLAND Lake Geneva

Geneva

0 miles 10

The rings
The tunnels are circular, and their depth below the surface ranges from 330 to 574 feet (100 to 175 m).

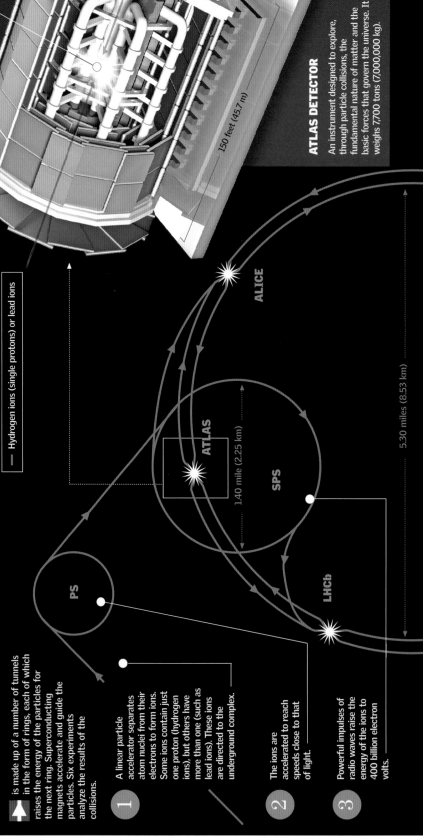

Collision of particles

7.9 feet (2.9 cm)

150 feet (45.7 m)

ATLAS DETECTOR
An instrument designed to explore, through particle collisions, the fundamental nature of matter and the basic forces that govern the universe. It weighs 7700 tons (7,000,000 kg).

The Complex

is made up of a number of tunnels in the form of rings, each of which raises the energy of the particles for the next ring. Superconducting magnets accelerate and guide the particles. Six experiments analyze the results of the collisions.

— Hydrogen ions (single protons) or lead ions

ALICE

ATLAS

SPS

PS

LHCb

1.40 mile (2.25 km)

5.30 miles (8.53 km)

1 A linear particle accelerator separates atom nuclei from their electrons to form ions. Some ions contain just one proton (hydrogen ions), but others have more than one (such as lead ions). These ions are directed to the underground complex.

2 The ions are accelerated to reach speeds close to that of light.

3 Powerful impulses of radio waves raise the energy of the ions to 400 billion electron volts.

Big Bang

The Large Hadron Collider, by obtaining data concerning elementary particles and fundamental forces, will make it possible for us to learn the properties of the universe a fraction of a second following the big bang, the great initial explosion of the universe.

A Record of the Collision

The particles that collide at high energy produce many elementary particles that exist for only millionths of a second, and they must be detected and analyzed in that short amount of time.

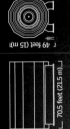

CMS

— Muon
— Electron
— Photon
— Charged hadron
--- Neutral hadron

Muon detector

Superconductor magnet

Hadron calorimeter

Electromagnetic calorimeter

Collision of particles

Silicon tracker

Entry of the particles that will collide.

Large Hadron Collider

In the LHC, either high-energy protons or high-energy lead ions collide against each other. Upon breaking apart as a result of the collisions, fundamental particles are generated in millionths of a second.

17 miles (27 km)

Streams of billions of now very highly energized ions are introduced into the LHC accelerator, some in one direction and others in the opposite direction. Superconducting magnets then increase their energy tenfold before particles are made to collide with each other.

CMS Detector

This instrument, which weighs 13,800 tons (12,500,000 kg), is designed to analyze the particles (such as photons, muons, and other fundamental particles) that are generated between protons at extremely high energies and to determine their mass, energy, and speed.

Muon detector permits the detection of this fundamental particle and allows for the measurement of its mass and velocity.

49 feet (15 m)

70.5 feet (21.5 m)

Superconducting magnets Cooled to almost absolute zero (about −459° F, or −273° C) with liquid nitrogen, the magnets are the largest that have ever been built. They impart high energy to the particles and guide them.

Silicon tracker It tracks charged particles and measures their speed and mass.

Electromagnetic calorimeter precisely measures the energy of lightweight elementary particles, such as electrons and photons.

Hadronic calorimeter records the energy of the hadrons and analyzes their interaction with atomic nuclei.

Entry of the particles that will collide.

Glossary

Alphanumeric

Made up of letters, numbers, and other characters.

AM

In telecommunications, amplitude modulation (AM) is the linear modulation of a wave that carries information. AM works by varying the amplitude of the wave in relation to the variations of information being sent.

Amino Acid

Type of molecule that contains a carboxyl group (-COOH) and a free amino group (-NH2). It is generally represented as NH2-CHR-COOH, where R is a radical or a side chain typical of each amino acid. Many amino acids build proteins.

Amplitude

In wave mechanics, the amplitude of a wave is its maximum value, both positive and negative. The maximum positive value is known as the peak, or crest, and the negative value is the trough, or valley.

Analgesic

Any medical or paramedical procedure that relieves or eliminates pain. Although the term is sometimes used to describe any substance or mechanism that relieves pain, it usually refers to a group of drugs from a number of chemical families that relieve or eliminate pain in various ways.

Antipyretic

Drug that reduces fever. Antipyretics include acetylsalicylic acid (aspirin), dipyrone, and paracetamol. The term comes from the Greek prefix anti-, meaning "against," and pyr, meaning "fire," or "fever." Antipyretics tend to be drugs that treat fever symptomatically; that is, they do not act on the underlying cause of the fever.

Artery

In anatomy, a blood vessel that carries blood away from the heart to the rest of the body. Arteries are membranous, elastic ducts with diverging branches that distribute throughout the body the blood expelled from the ventricular cavities on each systole.

Atomic Number

The number of protons found in the nucleus of an atom. It is traditionally represented by the letter Z. The atomic number uniquely identifies a chemical element and represents a fundamental property of the atom: its nuclear charge.

Catalyst

Substance capable of accelerating or delaying a chemical reaction while remaining unaltered (it is not consumed by the reaction). This process is called catalysis. Catalysts do not alter the final energy balance of the chemical reaction; instead, they allow equilibrium to be reached at a faster or slower speed. In the natural world, there are biological catalysts, or biocatalysts, and the most important of these are the enzymes, although some ribonucleic acids also have catalytic capabilities.

Catheter

In medicine, a device that can be inserted into a body cavity or vein. Catheters allow injection of drugs, drainage of fluids, or access of surgical instruments.

Cell

Main structural and functional unit of living organisms. The term comes from the Latin word *cellula*, meaning "small compartment."

CFC

Abbreviation for chlorofluorocarbon, which is the name of each of the compounds of saturated hydrocarbons obtained from substituting hydrogen atoms for chlorine or fluorine atoms. Because of their high physical and chemical stability, CFCs have been widely used as liquid refrigerants, extinguishing agents, and aerosol propellants. Their use has been prohibited by the Montreal Protocol because they destroy the ozone layer of the stratosphere, 30 miles (50 km) above sea level.

Chromosome

Long molecular strand within the central nucleus of a cell that contains genetic material. Each chromosome is made up of a single macromolecule of DNA with associated proteins. The number of chromosomes is constant for any given species. Humans have 46 chromosomes.

Convection

Convection is one of three ways to transfer heat: it does so by transporting matter between areas with different temperatures. Convection occurs only in fluids (which include gases). When a fluid is heated, its density is reduced and it rises upon being displaced by cooler portions of the fluid. These portions in turn are heated, repeating the cycle. The result is heat transfer by means of portions of the liquid ascending and descending.

CPU

Abbreviation for central processing unit. This component executes program instructions and controls the functions of the different components of a computer. It is usually integrated into a chip called a microprocessor.

Diffraction

In physics, diffraction refers to phenomena associated with wave propagation, such as the spreading and bending of waves when they meet an obstacle. Diffraction occurs with all types of waves, whether they are sound waves, waves on the surface of a fluid, or electromagnetic waves, such as light waves and radio waves. In the electromagnetic spectrum, the lengths of X-ray waves are similar to the interatomic distances within matter. Therefore, the diffraction of X-ray waves is used as a method to explore the nature of crystalline structures. This technique allowed for the discovery of the double helix structure of DNA in 1953.

Diode

Device that allows an electric current to flow in one direction. Below a given difference of potential, a diode behaves like an open circuit (that is, it does not conduct), and above it the diode behaves like a closed circuit, with very little electrical resistance. Because of this behavior, diodes are usually called rectifiers, as they can convert alternating current to direct current.

DNA

Abbreviation for deoxyribonucleic acid. This is the primary chemical component of chromosomes and the material from which genes are made. Its function is to provide instructions needed to construct a living organism that is identical to the original (or almost identical, such as when it combines with another chain, as in the case with sexual reproduction). DNA is a polymer whose monomers are made up of a phosphate group, a deoxyribose, and a nitrogen base. These four bases are adenine (A), guanine (G), cytosine (C), and thymine (T). The DNA structure is a long chain of nucleotides in the shape of a double helix.

Electromagnetic Radiation

Combination of electric and magnetic fields, oscillating and perpendicular to each other, that propagates through an area, transporting energy from one place to another. As opposed to other types of waves, such as sound, which need a material medium to propagate, electromagnetic radiation can travel through a vacuum.

Enzyme

Biomolecule that catalyzes chemical reactions. The term comes from the Greek word *enzyme* meaning "in yeast." Enzymes are proteins. Some RNA fragments are also able to catalyze reactions related to the replication and maturation of nucleic acid.

EVA

Abbreviation for ethylene vinyl acetate. It is also known as foam rubber. EVA is a thermoplastic-type polymer that is weather resistant and chemical resistant. It has low water absorption, is environmentally friendly, and can be thrown away, recycled, or incinerated. Applications include school supplies, footwear, set design, and handicrafts. It can be washed, and it is nontoxic.

FM

In telecommunications, frequency modulation. It is the process of coding information in a carrier wave, either in digital or analog form, by instantaneous variation in its frequency according to changes in the input signal.

Frequency

In wave mechanics, the number of oscillations (or complete cycle) of a wave per unit of time (generally per second). The average human ear can perceive frequencies between 20 and 20,000 hertz (cycles per second).

Gene

Basic unit of inheritance in living organisms. Molecularly, a gene is a linear sequence of nucleotides inside a DNA molecule that contains all the necessary information to synthesize a macromolecule with a specific cellular function. Genes are found inside every chromosome and occupy a specific location known as a locus. The set of genes in a species is called its genome.

GMO

Abbreviation for genetically modified organism, an organism whose genetic material has been deliberately designed or altered. The first GMOs date back to the 1950s, when commercial strains of yeast were modified through radiation. The genetic modification of organisms is an issue of great controversy. Environmental organizations such as Greenpeace warn that the risks of GMOs have not yet been fully investigated and that GMO crops can escape control as they disperse through the action of wind and birds, thus polluting native crops. On the other hand, supporters of GMO development argue that this type of technology can alleviate world hunger and reduce the impact of certain sicknesses (for example, it is possible to grow enriched rice that can prevent infectious disease, or cows can produce vaccines or antibiotics in their milk). Because of public pressure on this issue, legislative bodies in many countries are taking it into consideration and mandating, for example, explicit labeling of foods that contain GMO soy or corn as an ingredient.

GPS

Abbreviation for Global Positioning System, a system that can determine the precise location, within inches, of a person, car, or ship anywhere in the world. GPS utilizes a network of 24 main satellites with synchronized orbits to cover the entire surface of the Earth.

Graffiti

Letters or images scrawled on private or public property, such as walls, cars, doors, and street fixtures. In everyday language, the term also includes what is known as vandalism—in other words, signs, usually with political or social messages, painted without the property owner's consent. Sometimes slogans that became popular using these techniques have also been called graffiti, such as the ones that appeared during the revolts of May 1968 in Paris: "Power to the imagination" and "Beneath the pavement is the beach."

Hardware

The physical parts of a computer. Hardware includes electronic and electromechanical devices, circuits, cables, cards, boxes, peripherals, and other physical elements related to a computer.

Hertz

The unit of frequency of the International System of Units. The hertz is named after the German physicist Heinrich Rudolf Hertz, who discovered the transmission of electromagnetic waves. One hertz (Hz) represents one cycle per second, where a cycle is the repetition of an event.

Logarithm

In mathematics, a logarithm is the inverse function of an exponential function. Thus, the logarithm to base b of a number x is the exponent to which the base has to be raised to obtain the given number. For the equation $b^n = x$, the logarithm is a function that gives n. This function is written as $n = \log_b x$.

Macromolecule

Molecule with large molecular mass and high numbers of atoms. Macromolecules are generally the result of the repetition of one or a small number of minimal units (monomers) that make up polymers. They can be organic or inorganic, and many macromolecules are important to the field of biochemistry. Plastics are a type of synthetic organic molecules.

Microprocessor

Highly integrated set of electronic circuits used for computational calculations and controls. In a computer, this is the central processing unit (CPU).

Modulation

In telecommunications, the set of techniques that convey information in a carrier wave. These techniques allow more efficient use of communication channels, thereby facilitating the simultaneous transmission of information while protecting it from possible interference and noise.

Monomer

Small molecule that may become chemically bonded to other monomers to form a polymer. The term comes from the Greek words *mono*, meaning "one," and *meros*, meaning "part."

NTSC

The analog television encoding and broadcast system developed in the United States around 1940. It is named for the committee that developed it, the National Television Standards Committee. The NTSC standard is currently in use throughout most of North and South America and in Japan and India, among other countries.

OCR

Abbreviation for optical character recognition. It is a type of computer software designed to translate images of a text and store them in a format compatible with word-processing programs. In addition to the text itself, it can also detect the format and language.

PAL

Color-encoding system used in the broadcast of analog television systems in most of the world, PAL stands for phase alternating line. Developed in Germany, it is used in most African, Asian, and European countries, as well as in Australia and some Latin American countries.

Photoelectric Cell

Also known as photovoltaic cell, an electronic device that is sensitive to light and that can produce electricity from light. A group of photoelectric cells is called a photovoltaic panel, a device that converts solar radiation into electricity.

Polymer

Organic macromolecule composed of smaller molecules called monomers. The term is derived from the Greek words *polys*, meaning "many," and *meros*, meaning "parts."

Praxinoscope

Optical device invented in 1877 by Émile Reynaud. It used a strip of pictures placed around the inner surface of a series of spinning cylinders. A system of mirrors allowed the viewer, looking down into the cylinders, to experience the illusion of motion. In 1889, Reynaud developed the Théâtre Optique, an improved version capable of projecting images on a screen from a longer roll of pictures. This precursor to animation was soon eclipsed in popularity by the photographic film projector of the Lumière brothers.

Propellant

In aerosol spray cans, the propellant is the gas used to expel substances. CFCs were often used until it was discovered that they had negative effects on the atmosphere's ozone layer. Another propellant used in aerosol containers is butane.

Prostaglandin

Any member of a group of substances derived from fatty acids containing 20 carbon atoms. They are considered cellular mediators with a variety of effects that are frequently in opposition. The name "prostaglandin" derives from prostate gland. When prostaglandin was first isolated from seminal fluid in 1936, it was believed to be part of the prostatic secretions. In 1971, it was determined that acetylsalicylic acid could inhibit the synthesis of prostaglandins. The biochemists Sune K. Bergström, Bengt I. Samuelsson, and John R.

Vane jointly received the 1982 Nobel Prize for Physiology or Medicine for their research on prostaglandins.

Recycling

Process of reusing parts or elements of an object, technology, or device that can still be used, despite belonging to something that has already reached the end of its useful life.

Semiconductor

Substance that behaves like a conductor or an insulator depending on the surrounding electric field. Silicon is used to create most semiconductors. Other semiconductor elements are germanium, selenium, tellurium, lead, antimony, sulfur, and arsenic.

SMS

Abbreviation for short message service. Usually called text messaging, SMS is a means of sending short messages to and from mobile phones, landline phones, and other handheld devices. SMS was originally designed as part of the GSM (global system for mobile communications) standard but is now available on a wide range of networks, including 3G (third-generation) networks.

Software

The set of programs and procedures that enable a computer to perform specific tasks. The term is used in contrast to the physical components of the system (hardware).

Specific Weight

Weight per unit volume of a material. In the United States, it is measured in pound-force per cubic foot (lbf/cu ft). In the metric system, it is measured in kgf/cu m, and in the International System of Units, it is measured in N/cu m.

Stroboscope

Instrument used to make a cyclically moving object appear to be stationary or slow moving. It allows turning lights on and off at a given interval any number of times. This device was used on record turntables as an indicator that the turntable was revolving at the right speed.

The stroboscopic effect is what creates, for instance, the feeling of movement in a cartoon.

Telecommunications

Technique that allows the transmission of a message from one point to another, usually bidirectionally. The term is derived from the Greek word *tele*, meaning "distance." The term encapsulates all forms of long-distance communication (radio, telegraph, television, telephone, data transmission, and computer networks).

Thermodynamics

Branch of physics that studies energy—the way it is transformed into its various manifestations, such as heat, and its capacity to produce work. It is closely related to statistical mechanics, from which one can derive many thermodynamic relationships. Thermodynamics studies physical systems at the macroscopic level, whereas statistical mechanics usually describes the same phenomena at the microscopic level.

Toner

Also known as "dry ink" because of its functional similarity to ink, toner is a fine powder, usually black, that is deposited on the paper to be printed by way of electrostatic attraction. Once the pigment adheres, it binds to the paper by applying the necessary pressure or heat. Because there are no liquids involved, the process was originally called xerography, from the Greek word *xeros*, meaning "dry."

Transgenic

See GMO.

Transistor

Semiconductor electronic device used to amplify electric currents, generate electric oscillations, and perform modulation, detection, and switching functions. Its name is a combination of the words "transfer" and "resistor."

Trigonometry

Trigonometry, which in Greek means "triangle measure," is a branch of mathematics that studies angles, triangles, and the relationships between them (trigonometric functions). There is an enormous number of applications of trigonometry. For example, the technique of triangulation is used in astronomy to measure the distance to nearby stars and in geography to measure distances between landmarks; it is also used in satellite navigation systems.

Tungsten

Tungsten, also called wolfram, is a chemical element that has the atomic number 74 and belongs to group 6 of the periodic table of elements. Its symbol is W, and it is the only chemical element with two common names. Tungsten is a scarce metal that is found in certain minerals located in the Earth's crust. It is steel-gray in color, is very hard and heavy, and has the highest melting point of all the elements. It is used in light-bulb filaments, electrical resistors, and (when alloyed with steel) tool manufacturing.

Vein

In anatomy, a vein is a blood vessel that carries blood from the capillaries toward the heart. There are more veins in the human body than arteries, and the precise locations of veins vary much more from person to person.

Wavelength

In wave mechanics, wavelength is the distance, measured in the direction of the propagating wave, between repeating units of the propagating wave at a given frequency, such as peaks or adjacent valleys.

Zoetrope

Stroboscopic optical mechanism invented in 1834 by William George Horner. It consisted of a cylinder with vertical slits cut along the sides. The spectator looked through the slits at the pictures on the opposite side of the cylinder's interior. As the cylinder spun, the viewed images produced the illusion of motion. It was a very popular toy at the time and one of the precursors of cinematography. The term is derived from the Greek words *zoe* ("life") and *trope* ("turn").

Index